I0605362

AWN

Women of Achievement

Eleanor Roosevelt

Women of Achievement

Susan B. Anthony

Hillary Rodham Clinton

Marie Curie

Ellen DeGeneres

Nancy Pelosi

Rachael Ray

Eleanor Roosevelt

Martha Stewart

Women of Achievement

Eleanor Roosevelt

FIRST LADY

Janet Hubbard-Brown

CHELSEA HOUSE
PUBLISHERS

An imprint of Infobase Publishing

ELEANOR ROOSEVELT

Chelsea House
An imprint of Infobase Publishing
132 West 31st Street
New York NY 10001

Library of Congress Cataloging-in-Publication Data
Hubbard-Brown, Janet.
  Eleanor Roosevelt : First Lady / Janet Hubbard Brown.
    p. cm. — (Women of achievement)
  Includes bibliographical references and index.
  ISBN 978-1-60413-076-8 (hardcover)
  1. Roosevelt, Eleanor, 1884-1962—Juvenile literature. 2. Presidents' spouses—United States—Biography—Juvenile literature. I. Title. II. Series.

E807.1.R48H83 2009
973.917092—dc22
[B]

2008034643

Chelsea House books are available at special discounts when purchased in bulk quantities for businesses, associations, institutions, or sales promotions. Please call our Special Sales Department in New York at (212) 967-8800 or (800) 322-8755.

You can find Chelsea House on the World Wide Web at http://www.chelseahouse.com

Series design by Erik Lindstrom
Cover design by Ben Peterson

Printed in the United States of America

Bang EJB 10 9 8 7 6 5 4 3 2 1

This book is printed on acid-free paper.

All links and Web addresses were checked and verified to be correct at the time of publication. Because of the dynamic nature of the Web, some addresses and links may have changed since publication and may no longer be valid.

CONTENTS

Finding
Her Voice at 60

On April 12, 1945, Eleanor Roosevelt was attending a benefit at a club in Washington, D.C., when she was summoned to the telephone. She later wrote in *The Autobiography of Eleanor Roosevelt*: "I got into the car and sat with clenched hands all the way to the White House. In my heart I knew what had happened, but one does not formulate these terrible thoughts until they are spoken."[1] Her husband, Franklin Delano Roosevelt, the thirty-second president of the United States, had died in Warm Springs, Georgia, of a cerebral hemorrhage at age 63.

The White House had been home to the couple for 12 years, and during that time, Eleanor Roosevelt had become the most recognized woman in the world. When the news of her husband's death reached the public, American citizens went into shock and grief, for few had been aware of the declining health of the man who had been their president for so long. Although FDR, as he was referred to in print, had been in a wheelchair for more than 20 years after becoming paralyzed from polio, his handicap was not common knowledge. He had managed to create an illusion about his well-being with the aid of the media.

FDR's performance as the man who led his country through the Great Depression and World War II with tremendous confidence was anything but an illusion, however. He was the only president ever to be elected to a fourth term. (Today, the Twenty-second Amendment to the Constitution limits presidents to two terms.) Though he knew his health was failing, he deeply wanted to bring World War II to an end before he died. The first lady had encouraged him.

She had been thrust into politics alongside her husband, and by the time of his death, she was a respected stateswoman and political activist. She had revolutionized the role of the first lady. She was the first to drive her own car, travel by plane, travel alone, speak to a political convention, give a press conference, and earn her own money.

After hearing about her husband's death, Eleanor Roosevelt flew down to Georgia. Her daughter, Anna, was with her throughout the sad ordeal, but the Roosevelts' four sons were overseas. Franklin Jr. and John were in the Pacific war zone; Elliott, a brigadier general in the U.S. Army Air Forces, was flying missions over Germany; and James was in the Philippines. Only Elliott was able to make it home in time to attend his father's funeral. On April 13, the train carrying the president's body headed north from Georgia to Washington, D.C., where a public funeral would be held. Eleanor and Anna rode the train. As they traveled, they looked out at the crowds of people lining the tracks and waiting at stations and crossroads to pay their respects to their beloved leader. After the funeral, the family went to Springwood, Franklin's childhood home in Hyde Park, New York, where he was to be buried.

LOOKING BACK

After Vice President Harry Truman was sworn in as president, he often referred to Eleanor Roosevelt as the First Lady of the World. It had not always been that way. She had had to fight hard to transform herself from a painfully shy woman overwhelmed with feelings of inadequacy into a champion of rights for women and minorities. Even after finding her voice, she had been overshadowed by her husband's personality and her mother-in-law's need for absolute control.

Several events in her life had shaped her into the woman who stood as an icon to so many others. Both her father and her mother had died by the time she was nine. Her third baby, Franklin, died in infancy in 1909, leaving her bereft for a long time. In 1918, she learned that her husband was having an affair with her secretary, Lucy Mercer. His betrayal knocked the ground out from under her and changed the nature of their relationship. She had never been so humiliated—the relationship did not show up in print, but many of their friends knew, including Eleanor's cousin Alice, who had condoned the affair.

Eleanor wrote in her diary at the end of 1919 that "I do not think I have ever felt so strangely as in the past year . . . all my self-confidence is gone and I am on edge though I never was better physically I feel sure."[2] She took a long time to emerge from her depression. Slowly, she came to realize that she could not achieve fulfillment through someone else. It was the beginning of a new Eleanor, who would begin to focus more on the work she was destined to do.

The following year, Franklin, who had already served as a New York state senator and assistant secretary of the Navy, accepted the Democratic nomination for vice president, which set up a sense of dread in Eleanor, as she worried about having to turn into a social hostess, a role she despised. She did not have to deal with those fears, though, as the Democrats lost the election. Soon, however, another crisis occurred that turned her and her family's lives upside down.

During the summer of 1921, the Roosevelts and their children were vacationing at Franklin's family home on Campobello Island, which lies off the coast of northern Maine at the mouth of the Bay of Fundy. One day, 39-year-old Franklin took his three oldest children sailing and swimming. That night a sudden chill overtook FDR, and he went to bed early, exhausted. The following day he had a fever and had no strength in his legs; soon pain spread to his back and neck. What neither he nor his family realized was that he had contracted the dreaded poliomyelitis, a crippling disease.

Eleanor put all of her energy into caring for him, especially during the first few weeks when they could not get a nurse to Campobello. Soon, Franklin returned to New York for care. After several months, Franklin's mother, Sara, who had been the controlling force in the family since Eleanor and Franklin had married, insisted that her son be moved permanently to Springwood, away from the public eye. Eleanor was fiercely opposed to her husband's going into hiding, which was the fate of many disabled people in that era. She stood up to her mother-in-law for the first time, insisting that her husband stay in politics.

For seven years, Franklin Roosevelt tried to learn how to walk again, refusing to accept that he was a paraplegic. (Eventually both of them had to accept that he would not walk.) In the meantime, Eleanor was being groomed by her husband's political adviser, Louis Howe, to become a political organizer. She would become Franklin's eyes and ears in the future. She traveled many thousands of miles to represent him, and through those experiences, she realized that her deep interest in people, combined with an innate compassion and an ability to listen, gave her insights that FDR came to rely on.

LOOKING AHEAD

Eleanor was 60 at the time of her husband's death. When asked what she planned to do, she said, "The story is over."[3] She had surpassed everyone's expectations with her achievements. She had been the president's adviser and partner, spending 16 or more hours a day working for the country. Although her contribution was never publicly acknowledged by her husband, her biographer Blanche Wiesen Cook wrote in Volume 2 of her book titled *Eleanor Roosevelt*, "Little of significance was achieved without her input, and her vision shaped the best of his presidency."[4]

In 1938, on her fifty-fourth birthday, *The New York Times* ran two editorials celebrating her life and work. In joking that she talked a lot, the writer said:

> This is not in the tradition of the wives of former Presidents. But she [Eleanor Roosevelt] is so patently sincere and unpretentious in all she says and does, so ebulliently a part of every activity she undertakes, so good-humored even in the face of criticism, that she remains today one of the most popular women who ever lived in the White House. At 54 she could command a landslide of votes as Mrs. America. The question arose: "What sound reason can be advanced against a woman for President of the U.S.?"[5]

Two years later, Geoffrey T. Hellman, in a profile he wrote on the first lady for *Life* magazine, asked an editorial

Less than a month after her husband's death in 1945, former first lady Eleanor Roosevelt delivered a radio message to mark the Allied victory over Germany in World War II. During her time in the White House and afterward, Eleanor Roosevelt was a champion for the rights of women and minorities.

question about what would happen to Eleanor after the Roosevelt administration ended. He wrote, "This question has not existed before because no President's wife has ever before made a career of the First Ladyship. In any case, Mrs. Roosevelt can be counted on to solve the problem better than most ex-Presidents have solved the problem of what to do with ex-Presidents."[6]

In her autobiography, Eleanor told a different story. Writing about her years in the White House, she said, "It was almost as though I had erected someone outside myself who was the President's wife. I was lost somewhere deep down inside myself. That is the way I felt and worked until I left the White House."[7]

For the first time in her life, Eleanor was free of the influence of others and of the constraints put on her because she was a politician's wife. What she had not yet grasped was that within that freedom was the potential for her to transform the world, much as she had learned to transform herself. The question was, Would she have the courage and the stamina to go it alone?

A Storm-Tossed Childhood

Eleanor Roosevelt was born on October 11, 1884, into one of the "400 Families," a term used at the time to refer to what were considered the very best families in New York, all descended from great wealth. She was named Anna Eleanor after her mother, Anna, and her father, Elliott Roosevelt, whose nickname was "Ellie." Her mother was considered a great beauty, and her father was exceedingly charming and fun—when he was around.

Eleanor grew up feeling ashamed of what she perceived as her ugliness and lack of charm. The grave-faced little girl, who had to wear a back brace to correct a curvature of the spine, felt from an early age that she was a disappointment to her mother. Anna Roosevelt called her painfully shy daughter "Granny" because of her serious nature. At six, Eleanor was unusually tall for her age. She resembled the Roosevelts, not the traditionally beautiful Halls, her mother's family. Her mother stared at her one day and said, "You have no looks, so see to it that you have manners."[1]

Eleanor learned that she would receive positive feedback from her parents when she was nurturing. When her mother had a headache, Eleanor would rub her mother's head to make her feel better. After her brothers, Elliott Jr. and Hall, were born, however, Eleanor felt even more rejected by her mother, who openly adored her two little boys.

Her father, on the other hand, treated his namesake with great tenderness and love. His nickname for her was Little Nell because she reminded him of the little girl in *The Old Curiosity Shop*, a novel by Charles Dickens. In the story, Little Nell was very good and virtuous, and had a sad life. Eleanor's father became the center of her life, though he was too unstable to provide much of a foundation.

Although the Roosevelts had a house in Manhattan, they were rarely together as a family. Like other wealthy families, they summered with friends in Bar Harbor, Maine, or on Long Island, and Elliott and Anna traveled. They went to Europe for six months when Eleanor was a toddler, leaving her with her great-aunt and uncle. A feeling of isolation and abandonment remained with her the rest of her life. When her parents returned, the family spent two happy years in Hempstead, Long Island, but once they left there, Eleanor was not to know happiness for a long time.

AN ALCOHOLIC FATHER

Elliott began to drink heavily and, while warm and good-natured when sober, he changed into a violent and loud presence when on a drinking binge. Anna tried to think of ways to make him stop drinking, constantly reassuring him, but nothing worked. In 1890, the family traveled to health resorts in Germany, Austria, Italy, and France searching for a cure. While in Paris, Elliott met a woman and began to live openly with her. Anna was due to have a baby.

Elliott's brother, Theodore, whom Eleanor called Uncle Ted, was horribly upset about his brother's drinking and decided to get involved. He wanted to put Elliott in

ELEANOR'S ILLUSTRIOUS NAME

Eleanor and Franklin Roosevelt, fifth cousins once removed, were both descended from Claes Martenszen van Rosenvelt, who arrived in New York from the Netherlands in the 1640s. His two sons, Johannes and Jacobus, started the Oyster Bay and Hyde Park branches of the family. Eleanor was descended from Johannes's branch, while Franklin came from Jacobus's branch. The name has always been associated with power and wealth.

They were born into a WASP, or White Anglo-Saxon Protestant, culture. According to writer Joseph Alsop, who was born in 1910 into the same social realm as Eleanor and Franklin, "WASPs owned while almost everyone else rented, WASPs hired while others took jobs, and WASPs made loans while other borrowed."* This was true even into the 1930s. Many of the men were country gentlemen and did not have to earn money. They married women from their class, who often had great sums of money of their own.

The Roosevelt money came from the huge tracts of real estate acquired as far back as the 1700s, when land was bought from the Indians at a cheap price. Eleanor's great-grandfather Cornelius created a banking and investment business and left an institution and take his family away from him. Elliott went to an asylum in Paris, and Theodore brought a lawsuit that declared Elliott unable to take care of his property. Eleanor started to have headaches, aware that something terrible was wrong with her father, but she did not comprehend what was happening. In January 1892, Theodore sailed to Europe, where he persuaded his

$10 million to his four sons when he died. Even today that would be considered a vast fortune. The Roosevelt men were solid and industrious businessmen lacking in humor. The exception was Eleanor's grandfather, Theodore, a big, powerful man who was known for his grace, vitality, and responsibility. He left the business world and was one of the first to devote a great deal of time and energy to the poor. Eleanor's father, Elliott, whom she adored, was the third child of Theodore Sr. and Martha Bulloch, an outgoing and beautiful Southern belle. Elliott's older brother, Theodore, would become the twenty-sixth president of the United States.

Eleanor's mother, known for her beauty, was descended from the Livingston family, which played an important role in the formation of the new republic. One of her mother's ancestors signed the Declaration of Independence, another administered the oath of office to George Washington, and another became a Supreme Court justice.

---

* Joseph Alsop, *FDR: A Centenary Remembrance*. New York: The Viking Press, 1982, p. 11.

This family portrait was taken in 1890 when Eleanor Roosevelt *(right)* was six years old. Also pictured *(from left)* were her brothers, Elliott and Hall Roosevelt, and her father, Elliott. Eleanor's father doted on his young daughter, but he was an alcoholic who did not provide much of a stable family life. Eleanor's mother, Anna, was a great beauty who could not disguise her displeasure with her daughter's looks.

brother to go to a treatment center in the United States. Elliott felt completely beaten down. He entered the Keeley Center in Dwight, Illinois, for treatment of his addiction. After he left there, he went to Abingdon, Virginia, to work for his brother-in-law, Douglas Robinson. He felt exiled and angry. He wanted to see Anna, but she refused.

It was troubling and frightening for the eight-year-old Eleanor to have her father disappear. She began to blame her mother for her father's absence. The perceived split between Eleanor and her mother had to do with a lack of communication. Blanche Wiesen Cook explains in her biography of Eleanor that "Anna's disapproval of her daughter's solemnity reflected her own unwillingness to give in to the grave emotions that devastated her heart."[2] Anna could barely stand to look into Eleanor's eyes, which were full of accusations. Anna did not want to destroy the love Eleanor had for her father, and so she said nothing.

Eleanor, in the meantime, was not an easygoing child. Eleanor became sullen and grew stubborn and spiteful. She cried when told she had to attend parties. Several relatives had tried to teach Eleanor how to read and write, but by age seven she could do neither, so her mother brought in a tutor named Fredric Roser, whose teachings she resisted.

HER MOTHER'S DEATH

In 1892, Anna Roosevelt became ill with diphtheria. After several days, she died at age 29. Eleanor later wrote, "One fact wiped out everything else. My father was back, and I would see him very soon."[3] When Elliott arrived, he took "Little Nell" in his arms and told her that she and her brothers were all he had, and he promised that some day she would make a home for him. She was too young to understand that, instead of telling her she would be making a home for him, most fathers would have promised to make a home for their children. For Eleanor, the "secret of mutual understanding" between her and her father gave her hope.

Yet Eleanor felt completely abandoned. If her mother had not died so young, Eleanor would perhaps have come to realize that Anna had tried to protect her sensitive daughter. Naturally Eleanor had high hopes that she and her brothers would be able to move to Abingdon to live with Elliott, but her mother had been clear before she died that she wanted her children raised by her mother, Mary

Hall. Elliott did not strongly object, as he was still struggling with alcoholism.

For eight-year-old Eleanor, and her baby brothers, the move into their grandmother's dark brownstone on 37th Street in Manhattan required a major adjustment. Because Mary Hall's own children, now ranging in age from 18 to their mid-20s, were all living under her roof and were known for their wildness, she decided to be much stricter with her daughter's children. They had to bathe in cold water and were forced to wear old-fashioned clothes. There was to be no snacking, no games on weekends, and no reading in bed. Eleanor's grandmother spent most of her time in her room alone, coming down to make sure the servants were being strict with the children.

Though conditions at the big house were at times uncomfortable, Eleanor began to feel more secure than she ever had. She had a new sense of belonging. She thought of her two aunts, Maude and Pussie (Edith Livingston Hall), as her "early loves." Eleanor attended classes with Mr. Roser at classmates' houses, where she made friends and began to excel in her studies. She loved language, impressing her classmates with her writings. Trips to Oak Bluffs, her grandmother's estate in Tivoli, New York, were wonderful experiences. There, Eleanor could read to her heart's content and daydream. She was tutored in French and German and she studied piano for years. She was introduced to opera and theater. She took dance lessons, required of everyone in her class, and she also took ballet lessons.

In 1893, her baby brother, Hall, and three-year-old "Ellie" became ill with scarlet fever and diphtheria. Eleanor was sent to a friend's house in the country to protect her. Her father journeyed back to New York to check on his sons, but he did not go to visit his daughter. Eleanor received a telegraph from him explaining that while Hall, who was not yet two, was recovering nicely, it was likely that "Ellie" would die. His words were prophetic as the little boy passed away on May 29.

AN ORPHAN AT NINE

Elliott Roosevelt continued to make sporadic visits home. Eleanor would be filled with excitement, only to have all her hopes dashed if he didn't show up as promised. Once he left her out on the street holding the dogs while he went into a club to have a drink. Eleanor waited for six hours before the doorman finally took her home. Her grandmother decided to limit his visits. Eleanor and her father began to write letters to each other. Her letters were filled with longing; his were playful and full of advice. He wanted her to be loyal and brave and well-educated. He kept alive her dream of one day being able to live with him, which made her want to be the perfect girl.

He sent her a pony for her ninth birthday and urged Mrs. Hall to keep it in town so that Eleanor could ride several times a week. That fall, Elliott returned to New York and lived with his mistress. Eleanor and her governess saw him by chance riding in a hansom cab, and he offered to take his daughter to her sewing class. She went with him and, though terrified of his reckless way with the horses, she was too happy to be with him to let it show. That winter, Elliott returned to Abingdon, Virginia. He again wrote letters to his "Little Nell." Eleanor wrote back, telling of her adventures at Tivoli and Bar Harbor, where she spent the summer.

On August 14, 1894, Eleanor received a letter from her father, who wrote that he had been quite ill and that she should never forget that he loved her. Later that day, he was filled with delusions and had a terrible episode in which he jumped out of a parlor window. Hours later, he had a convulsion and died.

Many sorrows had struck the life of young Eleanor Roosevelt by the time this photograph was taken in 1895. Both her parents and one of her brothers had died by the time she was nine years old. She and her other brother, Hall, were sent to live with their maternal grandmother, Mary Hall.

Theodore Roosevelt went to Abingdon when he learned of his brother's death from their sister Corinne, who had gone there to try to help. Theodore could not imagine having Elliott buried next to his wife, Anna, at Tivoli, though that was what he had requested. Instead, Theodore arranged to have him buried at the family plot at Green-Wood Cemetery in Brooklyn. The Halls were overlooked, receiving a telegram that arrived too late for them to attend his funeral. When told of her father's death, Eleanor replied quietly, "I did want to see Father once more."[4] She was only nine years old.

The pain of loss was so great that Eleanor retreated more and more into the world of her imagination. She wrote, "While I wept long and went to bed still weeping, I finally went to sleep and began living in my dream world as usual. . . . From that time on I knew in my mind that my father was dead, and yet I lived with him more closely than I had when he was alive."[5]

Eleanor grew into a very tall and slender teenager, with blond hair and blue eyes. Her Uncle Theodore's wife, Edith, said, "Her teeth and mouth seem to have no future. But the ugly duckling may turn out to be a swan."[6] She had protruding teeth, which she hated all her life, and her chin was weak.

When Eleanor turned 14, she was allowed to go to Aunt Corinne's Christmas party. Eleanor was mortified to arrive wearing a child's party dress when all the other girls her age were in long, sophisticated gowns. Already considered homely, and hating herself for being so unattractive, she suffered a huge blow to her self-esteem. No one had bothered to teach her such basics as how to dress or how to present herself. The party, though, still had its moments. Eleanor danced with her fifth cousin once removed, Franklin Roosevelt, who told his mother later that he found her intelligent.

That was to be Eleanor's last dance for a while. When she turned 15, Mary Hall decided that her bizarre household was not appropriate for the teenager. Eleanor's Uncle "Vallie," her mother's brother, was difficult to handle, and Aunt Pussie, her mother's sister, was not considered the best example for the teenager. The solution was to send Eleanor to school in England. Eleanor was excited when she left to go abroad in 1899.

The Teen Years

Eleanor Roosevelt sailed to London with another sister of her mother's, Aunt Tissie (Elizabeth Livingston Hall), and her husband, Stanley Mortimer. She was to attend Allenswood, a finishing school on the outskirts of London. Many of the international elite sent their daughters to Allenswood, which took the education of women seriously in contrast to other schools. Allenswood, and a similar school in France called Les Ruches, were founded by a woman named Marie Souvestre. Eleanor's Auntie Bye (Anna Roosevelt Cowles) had attended the school and thought it would be perfect for Eleanor.

The students wore long black skirts, white ruffled blouses, and boaters (stiff hats with brims) when they went outdoors. Their days were programmed, and they had to be on time to everything. They made their own beds, and closets and bureaus had to be ready for inspection at a moment's notice. Whatever a student put on her plate had to be eaten. No matter the weather, the girls had to go for a walk after breakfast. Two hours of exercise were required. Eleanor thrived in the structured environment, a sharp change from the unpredictable days in New York.

She went out for field hockey and made the first team, one of the proudest moments in her life. Eleanor became physically healthier than she had ever been. Six feet tall, she had excellent posture and felt great. The headaches and chronic colds she had suffered most of her life disappeared. Perhaps what was most amazing to Eleanor was that her fears left her. She had sometimes been overcome with her fears—"of mice, of the dark, of imaginary dangers, of my own inadequacy," she wrote in her autobiography.[1]

Classes went throughout the day. Joseph P. Lash wrote in his biography *Eleanor and Franklin*, "To encourage concentration, the pupils were obliged to lie down on the floor after their midday meal and fix their minds for an hour on a single thought, which they later discussed at tea in French."[2] Girls who had proven their leadership skills were given privileges. One such privilege was to sit next to Souvestre at dinner, which was an education in itself. Eleanor, already fluent in French, could easily switch back and forth between English and French with her teacher. Souvestre chose her favorites based on their ability to interest and engage her. In her three years at Allenswood, Eleanor became the most favored student.

Eleanor had longed to be admired throughout her childhood, so much so that for a time she dreamed of becoming a singer. At Allenswood, all the positive attention allowed her to blossom.

"Sou," as Marie Souvestre was called by the girls, was 68 when Eleanor entered her school, which had an enrollment of 35 girls. She took a personal interest in Eleanor and became teacher, mentor, and parent to the girl who had been orphaned at nine. "Sou" had known both of Eleanor's parents, and her father's sister had been one of her students. Also, Souvestre's father had died when she was quite young, so she had a great empathy for her young charge. Over

MARIE SOUVESTRE

Born in France in 1830, Marie Souvestre was the daughter of Emile Souvestre, a well-known philosopher, novelist, and innovative educator. Among a group of radical thinkers in Europe, she founded and ran schools in France and England for the daughters of prominent U.S. and European families. Too much education for women was considered dangerous in Victorian society, the path to madness and sterility. These ideas shed light on how courageous Souvestre was to stand up to male disapproval, which, in her mind, "devoured with such ease the spirits of young women struggling to learn and to grow."*

One writer described her as a woman of striking presence, with silvery white hair, fine features, and penetrating eyes. She was short and stout. Souvestre gave lectures in history and literature, but perhaps most important was, according to Joseph Lash, "the intense enthusiasm she could inspire in the young for things of the mind, for courageous judgment, and for a deep sense of public duty."** She wanted her girls to think for themselves, as she had been taught to do by her father, and then time, she changed Eleanor's dress style and got her to stop biting her nails.

Eleanor was considered intelligent and attractive and a good friend to have. Given the nickname "Totty" by her classmates, she was popular and held in high esteem. Her favorite times were the evenings spent in Souvestre's study, where teacher and students read and talked. Souvestre liked to read aloud in French to the girls. Then, before bedtime,

to stand up for their ideals. She insisted that, to achieve and to survive in a world that denied them many rights, women had to learn to argue, to resist, and to be forceful. According to Lash, Eleanor was initially upset over her teacher's insistence that she break out of conformity, for it had been drilled into her that conforming was the way to win society's approval.

Some considered Souvestre too much of a political moralist, and more concerned with social justice than with analysis. She introduced Eleanor to the settlement movement. Settlements were privately funded inner-city institutions that provided social services to immigrants and the poor. Eleanor, during her three years under Souvestre's tutelage, absorbed how her revered teacher fought lost causes, often winning in the end. The underdog was to be championed.

*Blanche Wiesen Cook, *Eleanor Roosevelt, Vol. 1 1884–1933*. New York: Penguin Books, 1992, p. 104.
** Joseph P. Lash, *Eleanor and Franklin*. New York: W.W. Norton & Company, Inc., 1971, p. 80.

Eleanor Roosevelt was among the students shown here in 1900 at Allenswood, a private boarding school on the outskirts of London, England. (The girl in the center of the back row is believed to be Eleanor.) The headmistress of the school, Marie Souvestre, sought to teach the girls to break free from society's expectations.

all of the students assembled in the library. Mail was handed out, and announcements were made. Each student received a few words from "Sou," who either bestowed a kiss or held out her hand for a handshake.

Eleanor was selected to travel with Souvestre, and during her first Christmas abroad, they went to Paris. Her teacher turned out to be quite spontaneous and thought nothing of hopping off a train at a different destination from where she had planned. Eleanor had never known anyone like her. At the end of her second year at Allenswood, Eleanor was seen by her grandmother's neighbors sightseeing alone in Paris. They immediately reported what they saw to her grandmother, who insisted that she come home. Eleanor obeyed.

That summer she got into a fight with her Aunt Pussie, who told Eleanor that she was the ugly duckling of the family. Aunt Pussie continued her taunting by telling her niece about her father's awful last years. For the first time, Eleanor understood the secrets and mysteries surrounding her childhood, but the news devastated her. All she wanted to do was return to school. She pleaded with her grandmother, who said she would relent and let her go back if she could find a chaperone. Eleanor hired an Episcopal deaconess, who seemed respectable. Once they were on board the ship, though, Eleanor did not see her chaperone until the day they landed.

MAKING HER DEBUT

The tradition among the 400 Families in New York was to have young ladies make their debut into society at age 18, and Eleanor was no exception. She had wanted to remain at Allenswood for a fourth year and was heartbroken over having to return to New York to attend parties that held little or no meaning for her.

Souvestre wrote to her favorite student and friend after she left, "I am happy in the thought that these three years of such sustained and productive work on your part have also been a period of joy and rest for you and that they will, at the end of your adolescence and at the beginning of your youth, be a period you will look back to for a long time with satisfaction and serenity."[3] Eleanor requested a portrait of her teacher, which she kept on her desk for the rest of her life.

Eleanor returned to New York and the series of balls and parties that were a ritual for young society ladies to present themselves as a way of preserving the reign of the women in their line. Unlike her peers, however, Eleanor dreaded the events. She went immediately to Tivoli, her grandmother's summer estate, where she took charge of her younger brother Hall. After Allenswood, the atmosphere was gloomy. Her three uncles drank constantly. She most grieved the self-destruction of her beloved Uncle Vallie, whose alcoholic escapades and rampages were similar to her father's, though she never acknowledged that. She grew to hate alcohol and the way it changed people. She wrote that, by being around her uncles, she developed "an almost exaggerated idea of the necessity of keeping all of one's desires under complete subjugation."[4]

Her re-entry into home life at Tivoli, which was chaotic to say the least, did nothing to prepare her for the role of a debutante. Joy and the frivolous life were the furthest things from her mind as she tried to cope with the transition back into family life with the Halls. She dared not have friends come to Tivoli because of her Uncle Vallie, who on one occasion shot at guests with a rifle. Eleanor's grandmother, Mary, had become exhausted by her children and the responsibility of young Hall. Eleanor took over care of her brother, and when he went to Groton School, the alma mater of her Uncle Theodore, she wrote to him every day.

After that summer, Eleanor moved into the house on 37th Street, where she was mostly alone. Her Aunt Pussie, now 32, spent some time there, but her behavior was adolescent. Eleanor tried to run the house, dealing with Uncle Vallie's visits and Aunt Pussie's wild antics. It was a surprise when her grandmother decided to shut down the house. Eleanor went to live with her cousin and godmother, Susie Parish, on East 76th Street. She was invited to numerous dinner parties, and often found herself seated next to the host. She was an excellent conversationalist and had a wonderful ability to draw people out. Eleanor downplayed those qualities, feeling awkward that she was not more of a beauty. At this stage of her life, her biographer Cook wrote, "she could be cold, stubborn, and haughty as well as warm and tender. She hated deceit, and feared youthful alcoholic silliness."[5]

MEETING HER FUTURE HUSBAND

The first grand event of the social season was the horse show at Madison Square Garden on November 17, 1902. It was noted by newspapers that Eleanor sat in a box full of Roosevelt-Roosevelts. A favorite quote of the time was that "Roosevelts so often married Roosevelts because they never met anybody else."[6] She was with the family of James Roosevelt. Also seated in the box was Franklin Delano Roosevelt, James's younger half-brother. Franklin, whom she had met at Aunt Corinne's Christmas party when she was 14, was now a junior at Harvard. There is no record of how they perceived each other at the horse show, but as the season wore down, Franklin had attached himself to the elegant and willowy Eleanor. He was her height and charming and enthusiastic, much as her father had been. Cook wrote, "Franklin felt inspired. Eleanor felt hopeful."[7]

Eleanor hated the dances and regretted that she was not a more popular debutante. Franklin was the best part of the challenging season. On a train ride to their respective country homes in 1902, Eleanor and Franklin met up with each other. He insisted that she meet his mother, Sara Delano Roosevelt, who was still wearing mourning clothes after the death of her husband two years before. Eleanor was struck by her beauty and regal manner. Sara doted on her only child, and her life centered on him. When he went to Harvard College in Boston, she took a home nearby.

Franklin was careful about letting his mother in on any of his female interests, as he did not know how she would respond. When he was 20, he had proposed to 17-year-old Alice Sohier, but when her parents became aware of the proposal, they sent their daughter to Europe and the Middle East. She later admitted that, when Franklin confessed to her that he wanted to have at least six children because of his loneliness as an only child, she lost interest in him. Franklin's mother never knew of the proposal.

VOLUNTEER WORK

In the midst of all the parties, Eleanor had not forgotten her obligation to society, fostered during her years at Allenswood. She joined the Junior League for the Promotion of Settlement Movements, an organization made up of society women who wanted to do good works. The organization was formed in 1900 when a group of women were moved to action by the awful crowding, working conditions, and epidemics among the poor in New York. They wanted to create centers for social reform. Eleanor jumped right in, agreeing to teach exercises and dancing at the Rivington Street College Settlement on the Lower East Side of Manhattan. Eleanor, unlike her peers, took public transportation downtown, either the elevated train or the streetcar. She felt a little trepidation when walking through the area called the Bowery, observing the drunken men weaving out of the saloons. But she admired the children of the neighborhood and their enthusiasm. In 1903, she joined the Consumers' League, whose goal was to improve lighting and hygiene in workplaces. Such volunteer work provided a different kind of education for Eleanor as she saw how young girls and women were living in poverty.

Her work brought back memories of her father. When she was six, he had taken her with him to serve Thanksgiving dinners to children downtown, and he also took her along when he did volunteer service at the

After returning to New York to make her society debut, Eleanor Roosevelt also started to do volunteer work at the Rivington Street College Settlement on the Lower East Side of Manhattan. Through her work with the poor, Eleanor was beginning to realize the need for economic and political change.

Children's Aid Society. Against her family's wishes, she decided to continue. She liked doing good works, but she was also developing a deeper insight as she saw the need for economic and political change.

FIRST TASTE OF POLITICS

At 19, Eleanor felt pulled between the traditions of her mother and aunts and her own desire to change society. Her Aunt Bye, who had attended Allenswood before Eleanor, was setting a different kind of example in Washington as a highly respected intellectual. Theodore Roosevelt was now president of the United States, and the home of Aunt Bye, his sister, was often referred to as "the little White House." Eleanor grew to love her visits to the social and political realms of Washington. What she had always considered a man's world was, she realized, peopled by extraordinary women who were quite influential. Women were still not allowed to vote, but that did not prevent some of them from becoming powerful.

Franklin was in support of Eleanor's interests. He would often meet Eleanor on the Lower East Side after she had done her volunteer work, and he was shocked to see how the poor lived. The constant in Eleanor's life now was Franklin, and she wrote to him every night. They continued to keep their romance a secret. When he asked her to marry him in the fall of 1903, she accepted. She wrote years later, "When Franklin Roosevelt . . . asked me to marry him, though I was only 19, it seemed an entirely natural thing and I never even thought that we were both young and inexperienced. . . . I know now that it was years before I understood what being in love or what loving really meant."[8]

Franklin still hesitated to tell his mother, but Eleanor encouraged him to tell her so she would not feel she had been deceived. He finally agreed to do so. Sara was shocked and disapproving. She thought that they were too young—he was only 21—and that Eleanor was not the right girl for her son. They had to wait at least a year, she said, before they announced their engagement. Both agreed.

SIMILARITIES AND DIFFERENCES

Though sharing a common family pedigree, Franklin's background was quite different from Eleanor's. While Eleanor had felt like an orphan most of her life, Franklin was an adored only child. Unlike Eleanor, who had been fortunate enough to have been sent to a school where she was encouraged not to conform, Franklin went to Groton School in Groton, Massachusetts, which encouraged conformity and leaned toward "well-rounded if limited achievement" from its students.[9] What few knew was that Franklin had not been well-liked at his school. He adjusted his personality to try to fit in. His peers said he was a "feather duster"[10] because his newly developed charming and outgoing personality made him seem shallow.

And while Franklin had learned to maneuver through life with his charm, Eleanor had a rigid decorum that had been instilled in her by her grandmother and an exaggerated sense of duty and responsibility that was the result of having to grow up too fast. These differences, though, did serve to complement one another. At Harvard, Franklin did not make it into the Porcellian, a social club to which his father and Theodore Roosevelt had belonged. It was a devastating blow. Eleanor encouraged him to do better work, and to take his concerns and talents more seriously. He ran the school newspaper in his senior year.

A RESISTANT MOTHER

Sara tried to keep Franklin and Eleanor separated, even going as far as to take Franklin on a cruise for two months. Eleanor worked at courting her future mother-in-law because she genuinely wanted Sara to like her. She met most of the Delano tribe and was struck by the unity of the large family. She also appreciated seeing a family that had not thrown away its money through excesses as hers had. She was immediately accepted by Franklin's aunts and uncles, which warmed her heart. If only she could be successful with Sara.

Several other men were courting Eleanor when she said yes to Franklin. One, Howard Cary, who was a classmate of Franklin's at Harvard, wrote to him, "You are mighty lucky. Your future wife is such as it is the privilege of few men to have."[11] There were the naysayers, though, who thought that Franklin was not good enough for her. According to Cook, Eleanor's biographer, he was considered "frivolous and frothy" by some and "arrogant and deceitful" by others.[12] But Eleanor was deeply in love with Franklin, in whom she saw intelligence, tenderness, and attentiveness. Most of all, he reminded her of her father, and like her father, he needed her. She could once again focus on one person, giving him all her love.

Marriage to Franklin Roosevelt

Because of Eleanor's and Franklin's promise to Sara Roosevelt not to reveal their engagement for one year, family and friends remained unaware of their romance until December 1904. After the engagement was officially announced on December 1, the society papers celebrated Eleanor, and her closest relatives sent their well-wishes.

Eleanor and Franklin were married on March 17, 1905. Alhough this was the date of Eleanor's mother's birthday, the couple did not choose St. Patrick's Day as their wedding day because of her mother. Instead, they were accommodating Eleanor's Uncle Theodore, who would be in New York on that date to review the St. Patrick's Day Parade. Theodore Roosevelt had just been reelected to the presidency, and his inauguration had taken place on March 4.

Typically, Eleanor refused her uncle and aunt's offer to give her a White House wedding but chose instead to be married at the home of her cousin Susie Parish.

THE WEDDING

It was a great union of the two Roosevelt clans. Any tensions were dissolved for the day. Theodore considered Eleanor his favorite niece, and his daughter Alice was jealous. In recent months, Alice had been behaving outrageously in public. Eleanor knew that Alice gossiped about her, calling her boring and dowdy. Alice was also quick to criticize Franklin, referring to him as prissy. In the past, Edith, Theodore's wife, had purposely kept a distance from Eleanor, largely out of the fear that Elliott Roosevelt's alcoholism would affect her husband's reputation. Franklin's mother had resigned herself to the marriage but was not entirely supportive. She was prepared, though, to conduct her son's home life after his marriage.

Eleanor looked beautiful in the same lace veil and long train that her mother had worn at her wedding. She had on the engagement ring that Franklin had bought at Tiffany's, and she wore a long-sleeved, heavy satin dress and a pearl and diamond dog-collar necklace given to her by Sara. Two-hundred guests attended. Despite her differences with Eleanor, Alice was a bridesmaid. In fact, four of the six bridesmaids were from Eleanor's and Franklin's extended families. Eleanor's beloved Marie Souvestre, who had been invited to the wedding, was ill and died two days later.

Theodore arrived in time to give the bride away. Because of the St. Patrick's Day Parade, some guests never made it to the ceremony but were able to attend the reception. The moment the vows were said, Theodore rushed into the library for refreshments, followed by most of the guests. Within moments, the bride and groom found themselves standing alone. Her uncle told stories to the growing audience for more than an hour and then left. His daughter Alice said, "Father always wanted to be the bride at every wedding and the corpse at every funeral."[1]

The couple had a weeklong honeymoon alone at Sara's house in Hyde Park with the Scottish caretaker in charge. What Eleanor had not prepared for, and indeed had no way of preparing for, was how to create a place for herself in Franklin's and his mother's family life. With Franklin seated at one end of the long dining room table, and Sara at the other, Eleanor had little choice but to take a side seat. The symbolism was not lost on her. Eleanor began to realize that her mother-in-law was as difficult to please as her mother had been. Eleanor, seeing how much she and her new husband depended on Sara for financial help and advice, began to sink into that place of hurt she had known as a child. Within a short time, Sara had started to mock Eleanor's ignorance and incompetence as a wife.

Just after their honeymoon, Eleanor and Franklin had moved into an apartment in the Hotel Webster while he attended law school at Columbia University. Eleanor went about making life comfortable for him and for her brother, Hall, who visited often on holiday from Groton School. When the semester at Columbia ended, they went on an extended three-month honeymoon in Europe. It was a glorious time for the young couple. She learned that Franklin was troubled by dreams and nightmares, and she also noticed that he liked to flirt. They went to London for a short time and on to Paris, where they bought clothes, books, and prints. Eleanor loved Italy most, especially Venice. It was during this part of the trip that Eleanor had her first moment of pain as a wife. Believing it was beyond her ability, she had declined to take a mountain hike in

Eleanor Roosevelt wore the same lace veil and long train that her mother had worn at her wedding. Eleanor and Franklin Roosevelt were married on March 17, 1905, in New York City. Her uncle, Theodore Roosevelt, who had just begun his second term as president of the United States, gave the bride away.

Italy. Without trying to persuade his wife to come, Franklin headed off on the climb with others. So began a pattern—of Franklin's refusal to encourage Eleanor—one that would affect them for years to come.

Upon their return to New York, they moved into a house that Sara had rented for them. The couple had approved of the house ahead of time, but they were surprised to learn that Sara had furnished it herself and hired servants. Eleanor and Franklin were to live at Sara's house in New York and at Springwood, until their place was perfect. Eleanor went out of her way to please her mother-in-law but was basically ignored. Finally, she allowed herself to become completely dependent on Sara, and in the process lost all self-confidence. She blamed herself sometimes, for she had slipped into a lifestyle in which she had no responsibilities. In the beginning, Eleanor had thought she could create a relationship with Sara similar to the one she had enjoyed with Marie Souvestre. Sara, however, wanted no part of an independent young woman.

With their combined trust income, the young couple could have lived comfortably on their own, although not

(continues on page 44)

IN HER OWN WORDS

Eleanor Roosevelt would learn to overcome the lack of self-assuredness that plagued her during her early childhood and in the first years of her marriage. As she wrote in *This Is My Story* in 1937:

No one can make you feel inferior without your consent.

THE ROOSEVELT CHILDREN

Eleanor Roosevelt had six children in 10 years—Anna in 1906; James in 1907; Franklin, who was born and died in 1909; Elliott in 1910; another son the Roosevelts named Franklin in 1914; and John in 1916. Edna Gurewitsch, a Roosevelt family friend, said, "I think she was totally inept when it came to dealing with children. She relied on her mother-in-law and on the various governesses and was so unsure of herself not only because she was an unsure person at the time, but she had never experienced mother love."*

Blanche Wiesen Cook, Eleanor's biographer, speaking in an interview, explained that Eleanor was an unhappy mother and an unhappy wife early in her marriage. She said, "She had never known what it was to be a good mother. She didn't have a good mother of her own. And so there's a kind of parenting that doesn't happen."** There were nannies and servants, and as with the children of other upper-class families, the parents came in to say goodnight. By the time the boys were 12, they were sent off to boarding school.

Franklin Roosevelt was not a model parent either, but it was typical for the mother to take the blame. Historian Geoff Ward said, "Her husband was not a very good father, and expected her and his mother to do all the parenting, and he was sup-posed to come home and have fun with the kids. And he did. They adored him. But when that was over, he wasn't really very interested in helping them much. And I think the children suf-fered from the problems both their parents had."***

Once their father became president, the Roosevelt children were constantly in the news. James had tax problems, and Elliott could not seem to hold a job. Franklin Jr. was a speed demon. John poured a bottle of champagne into a top hat belonging to the mayor of Cannes, France. None of these episodes would have amounted to much were their parents not in the spotlight. Their mother's response? "There's a bond between us," she said, "and right or wrong, that bond can never be broken. . . . No one lives up to the best of themselves all the time, and nearly all of us love people because of their weaknesses rather than because of their strengths." [†]

All of the Roosevelt children wound up having troubled lives. They struggled with feelings of jealousy, financial difficulties, and failed marriages. Among the five children, there were 19 marriages. Franklin Jr. was married five times. After he lost the election for New York attorney general in 1954, Lou Harris found him crying openly and asked what was wrong. Franklin said it was too much to bear, "to be the son of Franklin D. Roosevelt and Eleanor Roosevelt. It's so much to live up to. And I guess I've not done it." [††]

As the children matured, it became clear that they resented their public mother who gave her all to her friends and to complete strangers. She seemed a better mother to her grandchildren than she had been to her own children. Cook, however, saw her differently. "She was a very devoted mother," she said. "One of the reasons she worked to the very end of her life was she was constantly bailing her children out." [†††]

American Experience: The Presidents—FDR. PBS/WGBH, 1994.
**American Experience: Eleanor Roosevelt.*
***Ibid.
[†]Candace, Fleming, *Our Eleanor: A Scrapbook Look at Eleanor Roosevelt's Remarkable Life.* New York: Atheneum Books for Young Readers, 2005, p. 81.
[††]*American Experience: Eleanor Roosevelt.*
[†††]Ibid.

(continued from page 41)

at the same high standard of living. Eleanor, though, was never able to persuade her husband to break free from his mother's authority. In his mind, life was perfect. It was easy for him to ignore the tensions between his mother and his wife, for he had learned as a child to ignore anything that was difficult or painful. While it worked in many situations, his indifference made Eleanor feel abandoned.

During these early years of marriage, Eleanor gave birth to four children in rapid succession: Anna was born on May 3, 1906; James was born on December 23, 1907; and Franklin arrived on March 18, 1909. He had a weak heart and died at seven months, which devastated Eleanor. As would become her pattern as far as her children were concerned, she blamed herself. She was convinced that there must have been something she could have done to prevent his death. Eleanor went through a depression afterward and kept a photograph of him by her bed for the rest of her life. A fourth child, Elliott, named after Eleanor's beloved father, was born on September 23, 1910.

With Sara in control, and nannies to care for the children, Eleanor fell into a depression. She grew to call these periods her "Griselda" moods. Griselda was a peasant girl in medieval stories written by the poet Geoffrey Chaucer and others. She was offered title and comfort by a marquis if she agreed to be completely obedient for the rest of her life. Griselda agreed, remaining sweetly servile no matter what was done to her by those who were stronger.

ENTRY INTO POLITICS

Franklin worked for a law firm but was bored. He stayed out late at night, playing poker or mingling with friends at clubs. Eleanor, who hated drinking, was upset when he returned. She tried to bury herself in the details of child care, though she did not feel needed. She focused on entertainment and homemaking.

In 1910, the Reform Democrats in New York were looking for new faces, in their effort to end the rule of a party leader they did not like. The Roosevelts, including President Theodore Roosevelt, were traditionally Republican. The Democratic leaders turned to the 28-year-old Franklin as a possible candidate to run for a State Senate seat. While Eleanor took her children to Campobello off the coast of Maine, where Franklin's mother had a summer home, Franklin toured the Senate district, speaking to the people. Though he gave superficial answers, which came easily to him, he could think on his feet and spar with the crowd. Later, Eleanor joined him on the campaign trail. He won the seat, and the Democrats won statewide for the first time in 18 years.

AN EXCITING NEW LIFE

The young couple moved to Albany, the seat of government in New York. The new circumstances presented Eleanor with a decision. According to Cook, her biographer, Eleanor understood that "she could emerge from her depression and fulfill her lifelong wish to be useful to someone she loved, or remain withdrawn and morose and be a terrible liability to her husband's new career."[2] She chose the former.

The couple lived away from Sara, which gave Eleanor her first taste of domestic freedom. Unlike her mother-in-law, Eleanor found politics fascinating, and she jumped in with both feet to help her husband. In assisting him, she found a place for herself that had nothing to do with society or having children. All of the training she had received

In 1910, the Reform Democrats recruited Franklin Roosevelt to run for a State Senate seat in upstate New York. Here, Eleanor and Franklin Roosevelt wait at a train station during a campaign trip. Roosevelt won the election, and the family moved to the capital, Albany.

as a student at Allenswood could now be put to use, and as a result, Franklin began to rely on her to tell him what the people wanted.

He had an unbounded enthusiasm for their new life and quickly made a name for himself as a political warrior, learning through his mistakes. Eleanor attended debates, called on the wives of politicians and newspapermen, and involved herself in any situation related to connecting with the people. There was no political role for her, for at the time women were denied ambition and self-fulfillment. Eleanor was careful to explain that her work was for her husband, and she came to be greatly admired.

During these years, when Franklin's political future was still unclear, he met a witty wreck of a man named Louis McHenry Howe. A political reporter and a brilliant strategist, Howe attached himself to Franklin Roosevelt, believing he had an outstanding career ahead of him. Howe's constant smoking, rumpled appearance, and scrawny physique, though, put off Eleanor Roosevelt. Howe did help Franklin get reelected, however, which was in his favor.

In the 1912 election, Franklin Roosevelt had also been an ardent supporter of Woodrow Wilson, who was running for president. After Wilson was elected, FDR was appointed assistant secretary of the Navy, which thrilled him. Franklin was headed in the direction he sought— Theodore Roosevelt, too, had been assistant secretary of the Navy.

During Wilson's inauguration, Eleanor watched a suffrage parade with amusement. The parade was the largest in U.S. history. She wrote to a friend: "The suffrage parade was too funny and nice fat ladies with bare legs and feet posed in tableaux on the Treasury steps!"[3] She, like many women, still believed that men were superior, especially when it came to politics. As for racism, Eleanor was quite oblivious at the time, and she was in for a much less amusing jolt soon after the family moved to Washington. Her husband's boss criticized her for bringing white servants to Washington, saying that only blacks should do servants' work. Eleanor was appalled at his prejudice. There was a kind of innocence about the young couple in those days that was about to change.

Life-Changing Events

Eleanor and Franklin Roosevelt were separated for the first time on their wedding anniversary when Franklin was sworn in as assistant secretary of the Navy on March 17, 1913. For the summer, Eleanor moved the family and servants to Campobello. It had been a great year for them, and Eleanor's biographer Blanche Wiesen Cook wrote, "They were allied, tender, generous and loving with each other, expectant and happy."[1]

Eleanor and the family were back in the nation's capital by the autumn of 1913. Washington was an exciting place to be. The Democrats were in charge for the first time in 16 years. Eleanor's Uncle Theodore had paved the way for them socially, as they inherited many of his friends and supporters. Tall and slender, with her thick hair worn in an upswept style, Eleanor was lovelier than she had ever been. Her routine included the tradition of "calling," visiting anywhere from 10 to 30 wives of politicians and Supreme Court judges daily. Because of this practice, she came to know practically everyone, looking for friends and allies. She kept a detailed journal and reported to her husband about it all. During this time, on August 17, 1914, Eleanor gave birth to a boy, and the Roosevelts gave him the same name as the infant who had died—Franklin Delano Jr. Less than two years later, on March 13, 1916, she had another son, John.

Louis Howe had become Franklin's assistant, and he never passed up an opportunity to promote his boss, to whom he was devoted. Eleanor held open-house luncheons, never knowing how many people Franklin would bring home. The couple became known for their dinners as well, and for their individual successes. Eleanor was held up as an example of the perfect political wife. Not only was she a splendid hostess, but she also had a brilliant mind.

WORLD WAR I

When World War I started in Europe in August 1914, the people of the United States were shocked and confused. Two vastly different camps of philosophy quickly emerged: that of Theodore Roosevelt and FDR, who wanted the United States to become involved, and that of the president, Woodrow Wilson, and his secretary of State, William Jennings Bryan, who wanted peace at all costs. Franklin tried to pressure the administration into creating a stronger Navy, especially after conflicts erupted in Mexico and Haiti. After a ship called the *Lusitania*, which was carrying passengers and weapons to England, was torpedoed in 1915 and more than 100 Americans died, Bryan resigned, and the United States took on a more aggressive stance.

During the 1916 presidential race, Wilson campaigned as the president who kept the country out of war, and he won reelection. But within months, on April 2, 1917, Wilson appeared before Congress to ask for a declaration of war. Eleanor was in attendance during Wilson's address and felt "the world rocking all around us."[2]

INNER WORLD MATCHING THE OUTER

The war created political changes and domestic changes. On a more personal level, it seemed to accentuate the individual character traits of the attractive couple. Eleanor helped to organize the Red Cross canteen and the Navy Red Cross. Some days she worked past midnight. "Duty first" was her motto. She delved into a world of suffering, as she helped to tend to injured soldiers returning home. Perhaps Eleanor was able to participate so much because the Roosevelts had 10 servants, a fact that came out in an article on the family's food-saving program during the war. The article, which appeared in *The New York Times*, left Franklin upset. It created a stir, and Eleanor would never again refer to her household.

One of Franklin's biographers, Joseph Alsop, wrote in his book *A Centenary Remembrance* that Franklin "loved the world and its pleasures."[3] Starting in 1909, Eleanor and Franklin had agreed that she would not interfere with Franklin's craving for fun and people as long as she did not have to endure alcoholic evenings with his acquaintances. By 1917, Eleanor's focus was on war activities, while Franklin's was on the nighttime wheeling and dealing that went on in private homes and clubs. Their family tradition of retreating to Campobello during summers was interrupted by Franklin's job, and from 1913 to 1917, Eleanor spent much more time there with the children than Franklin did. He was 35 and described as high-spirited and handsome. Women were drawn to his flamboyant personality.

BETRAYAL

In 1914, Eleanor hired a young society woman named Lucy Mercer as her social secretary. Eventually the two women became friends, and Lucy, who was cheerful and accommodating and 10 years younger than Eleanor, stepped in to dinner parties as an "extra," and even helped out with the Roosevelt children.

While Eleanor and the children were at Campobello during the summer of 1917, Franklin continued to write chatty letters to his wife. He did not hide his multiple social engagements from her, including evenings in the company of Lucy. Eleanor was worried, yet said nothing. When he was hospitalized with a throat infection, he asked her to come and she immediately went back to Washington. After two weeks, she returned to her family.

In the meantime, people had started to gossip about Franklin and Lucy Mercer, who showed up with him everywhere. Franklin also became good friends with Eleanor's first cousin Alice Roosevelt Longworth, who was known for her outrageous behavior. Eleanor's biographer Cook wrote, "It is clear that FDR did very little to protect his wife from gossip, did nothing significant to hide his affair, and went so far as to enlist many of their mutual friends in his relationship."[4]

Eleanor returned to Washington in November and over the next several months she and her husband saw little of each other. Eleanor put all of her energy into her Red Cross work, and Franklin traveled. She took a personal interest in the wounded soldiers and their families—bringing them fresh flowers, candy, and newspapers, along with her attention. From the soldiers and the families, she received many letters of thanks.

During the summer of 1918, Eleanor learned to drive, and from then on, she drove herself everywhere. She also learned to swim. As had been customary for the past few summers, she spent many weeks alone with her children at Campobello. She and the children also made several visits to Sara at Hyde Park. Her relationship with her mother-in-law had changed since the early, insecure years, and the two women had developed respect for each other. Sara clung to the traditions and ways of the aristocracy, even as Eleanor and Franklin began to think her old-fashioned.

Eleanor was with Sara in Hyde Park when a telegram arrived in September that announced that Franklin was sailing home from Europe with pneumonia and influenza. They needed to meet him with an ambulance and a doctor. The deadly Spanish influenza epidemic was spreading around the world—it would eventually kill millions of people. On Franklin's ship, many crew members had died and were buried at sea.

After getting her husband home, Eleanor unpacked his suitcase and discovered a packet of love letters written to him. They were from Lucy Mercer. It was clear that her husband was in love with another woman.

BROKEN-HEARTED

Eleanor went into total despair. Her fixed vision of what marriage should be was shattered. She confronted FDR and offered him a divorce. It was an extreme gesture, for divorce then was rare and considered shameful. Sara intervened, telling Franklin that she would disinherit him if he chose divorce. Sara was one of the richest women in America, so the loss would be substantial. He also had his five children to consider. Louis Howe stepped in and warned Franklin that divorce would mean the end of his political career. Franklin promised Eleanor that he would never see Lucy Mercer again.

He lied to Lucy and told her that Eleanor would not give him a divorce. Lucy quickly married a much older man, Winthrop Rutherford, which shocked Franklin. Eleanor was

The Roosevelt family posed for a photograph in 1919 at Sara Roosevelt's home in Hyde Park, New York. The children are *(from left)* Elliott, Franklin Jr., John, Anna, and James. Franklin's mother, Sara, is seated between Franklin and Eleanor. In many pictures from this period—shortly after Eleanor Roosevelt found out about her husband's relationship with Lucy Mercer—Eleanor did not look at the camera.

humiliated by the scandal. Though it was not published in newspapers, all of their friends knew, and many had helped to make it happen. The level of betrayal around her was enormous. Eleanor later admitted to close friends that she forgave Franklin but that she never forgot. Eleanor's biographer Cook wrote that the discovery of her husband's affair was "the moment that most profoundly changed her life."[5]

She could not eat. Photographs of her during this period show an underweight and dejected-looking woman with protruding teeth who rarely looked into the camera. She had headaches and had lost her will to forge ahead. Today, Cook believes, she would be said to suffer from anorexia. She went through a long period of introspection. Although Eleanor suffered a big loss of self-confidence, she did not stop trying to understand what had happened to cause such a disruption in her marriage. Much of the repair work was typical of any couple in a marital crisis. Franklin tried to spend more time with the children. Eleanor went to more parties with her husband and traveled to Europe with him. The war had just ended, and Eleanor was stunned by the devastation and the loss of lives. She dedicated herself to the fight for the League of Nations. She was also beginning to explore her own independence. While in Europe, Franklin went on a trip to Brussels and Cologne, but Eleanor was not allowed to accompany him. She was open about her resentment of a woman's place being on the sidelines. She was becoming vocal about her feelings. At the same time, Franklin's friends felt that his bitter disappointment in love helped to create new depths in him.

TURBULENT TIMES

The war had ended, but a sense of unease still pervaded the world and the nation. The Communists had taken over the Soviet Union, and a "Red Scare" had taken hold in the United States, as the government cracked down on radicals and other progressives. Women were continuing their push to get the vote. As Cook wrote, "For fifty years, in England and the United States, they [women] had picketed, marched, petitioned, demonstrated. They had been arrested, brutalized, and, when they conducted hunger strikes in prisons, force-fed."[6]

Another issue gripping the nation was the position of African Americans in society. As soldiers returned from World War I, those who had replaced them in jobs—mostly women and blacks—were fired. Cook wrote, "The benefits of the war to make the world safe for democracy were to be restricted to whites."[7] President Wilson's segregationist policies were about to be tested. Race riots turned 26 cities in the United States into war zones. Black citizens, many still in uniform, were lynched, and they began to arm themselves.

SUMMER OF DISCONTENT

In the summer of 1919, Eleanor Roosevelt would not be traveling to Campobello. She stayed with her husband through June in Washington, and then the couple spent part of July in Hyde Park. Eleanor's newfound determination to do things her way caused confrontations with Sara. They fought over the children, food, money, and more. Eleanor, insulted, grew angry.

On August 14, 1919—the twenty-fifth anniversary of her father's death—Eleanor's grandmother, Mary Hall, died. The death led Eleanor to focus on the women in her life and their overall unhappiness. She wondered most of all if her grandmother would have experienced more fulfillment if she had had a life of her own aside from her family. She did not feel uplifted either when she focused on the Delano women, who now seemed in Eleanor's eyes to be arrogant and overbearing. In the past, Eleanor had seen them as models of familial love and generosity. Her own aunts did not fare much better in her opinion of them, as she saw them as undeveloped.

"Out of her grief, she begins to compare her life to her grandmother's life," Cook said on a PBS program. "Her grandmother could have been a painter. Her grandmother could have done so much more than she did. And it's very clear to her that being a devoted wife and a devoted mother is not enough. And Eleanor Roosevelt decides she is going to do everything possible with her life. She's going to live a full life."[8]

She decided not to allow all of her interests to center on her husband and children. She determined through many hours of quiet contemplation that the life you live is your own. With that in mind, she took some sudden and bold steps. The first was to fire all her servants in Washington. She felt that they bullied her and that the final word on any issue was left to Sara.

That same month, a race riot occurred in Washington when white sailors went looking for two youths accused of "jostling" and insulting the wife of a naval officer. A white police officer was shot in self-defense. Groups of sailors and Marines pulled African-American men and women off streetcars and beat them. Hundreds were injured as whites and blacks attacked one another. Finally 2,000 supplementary troops were brought in, and the violence eased.

Eleanor was worried about Franklin's life being in danger, but she need not have. When she went to Washington, she saw that he was again the life of the party. She knew that Lucy Mercer attended many of the same parties. On the night she returned to Washington, the couple attended a party. As Franklin's attentions seemed elsewhere, Eleanor decided to head home. She realized too late that she had forgotten her key and so sat and waited for hours, asleep on their doormat, for her husband to come home.

The incident again demonstrated to Eleanor that she needed to care less about what her husband was doing and

(continues on page 60)

ELEANOR'S BEST FRIENDS

Until she was 35, Eleanor Roosevelt had not focused on friendship, but when she found herself completely alone on her birthday that year, she understood how lonely she was. In the years afterward, she formed several close friendships.

While campaigning with her husband in 1932, she developed a friendship with reporter Lorena Hickok. The friendship became a passionate one. Hickok had a profound influence on Eleanor's transformation from supportive wife to a political force. Hickok eventually retired from the newspaper business and worked for the Federal Emergency Relief Administration. In 1978, more than 3,000 letters that Eleanor had written to Hickok were discovered. They were later compiled into a book, *Empty Without You: The Intimate Letters of Eleanor Roosevelt*. Speculation about the nature of the friendship led many to believe that the two women had a romantic relationship.

Eleanor had an equally intense friendship with Earl Miller, a tall and handsome New York state trooper. In 1929, Franklin, then the governor of New York, appointed Miller to protect Eleanor, who had refused to be driven in the state-appointed car. She was 44, and he was 32. He gave her a horse and coached her in tennis. He taught her to dive and to shoot a gun. He stepped into family crises easily, taking the burden off Eleanor. Those who were close to her disapproved, concerned that the relationship had romantic overtones. Gossip followed them, but Eleanor ignored all of it. Her son James believed his mother had an affair with Miller, but there is no proof today.

Malvina "Tommy" Thompson, who became Eleanor's assistant and secretary in the late 1920s, was another "best friend." She was also her traveling companion. She had a wonderful ability to make Eleanor laugh. When Eleanor converted the Val-Kill Furniture Factory into a residence, she designed a special area for Thompson. After Thompson's death in 1953, Eleanor was bereft. Eleanor said that she "learned for the first time what being alone was like."*

Eleanor met Joseph Lash when he appeared before the House Committee on Un-American Activities, which was investigating Americans involved with Communism. Lash, 29, had just resigned from the American Student Union and was going through a difficult period. Intrigued by the earnest young man who spoke eloquently about students and their political leanings, Eleanor, 55, invited him to the White House. She was drawn to Lash and felt free to confide in him about her life. He was a sympathetic listener, and she could lavish her attention and tenderness onto him. She brought him together with Trude Pratt, who eventually became his wife. Eleanor helped Lash form Americans for Democratic Action, which lobbied for national health programs and affordable housing. Their lives continued to overlap professionally as he covered the United Nations for the *New York Post* when Eleanor was a delegate. In the 1950s he began the first of several books he wrote on the Roosevelts, winning a Pulitzer Prize for his book *Eleanor and Franklin*.

---

*Eleanor Roosevelt, *You Learn By Living: Eleven Keys for a More Fulfilling Life*, Louisville, Kentucky: Westminster John Knox Press, 1960, p. 85.

(continued from page 57)

more about her own needs. She was beginning to realize that she wanted to participate in work that was traditionally denied to women. She grew to hate Franklin's childhood homes and his mother's daily presence. Sara had taken over with the children and spoiled them in ways that Eleanor believed harmed their growth.

On her thirty-fifth birthday, Eleanor was in Washington and Franklin was heading to New Brunswick, Canada, to hunt with friends. She had no close friends of her own, no relationships with anyone who knew the inner workings of her heart and mind. It was a moment of truth for her, and again she decided that it was up to her to change what was wrong with her life. Later that month, she began to move in that direction, as she made her first contact with an organization seeking to improve working conditions for women. She volunteered to be a translator during the International Congress of Working Women.

BACK ON THE CAMPAIGN TRAIL

As President Wilson's term was coming to an end, Franklin Roosevelt was considering a run in 1920 to be either governor of New York or one of its U.S. senators. That June, he went alone to the Democratic convention in San Francisco, while Eleanor traveled with the children to Campobello; she took their oldest son, James, to Groton School, where he would follow in the tradition of his father, Uncle Hall, and Great Uncle Theodore Roosevelt. At the convention, though, the direction of Franklin's political career shifted. He was enlisted to be the Democrats' vice-presidential candidate, running on the ticket with James M. Cox, the governor of Ohio.

After winning the nomination, Franklin began an extended campaign. The crowds loved him as he crossed the West on a train. Eleanor went along for some of the campaigning, but did so begrudgingly. She tried to coach

Eleanor Roosevelt sat with her husband, Franklin, and her mother-in-law, Sara, for a 1920 photograph at the Hyde Park residence. That year, Franklin Roosevelt was the Democratic nominee for vice president, although the ticket was soundly beaten by the Republicans.

him on his speeches, but when night came the robust and unstoppable FDR liked to play poker and drink. Louis Howe continued to be Franklin's right-hand man, helping to "package" the man he predicted years before would be president of the United States. In earlier years, Eleanor had barely managed to tolerate the gnome-like man, but as the campaign wore on, she slowly developed a respect for him, and by the end of the journey they had become solid friends.

She found that she was drawn to the reporters who covered the campaign. They were smart and had a hearty style. They helped her to see the humorous side of life; when Franklin flirted with the women around him, they would tease her. They grew, in turn, to appreciate her warmth, generosity, and intelligence. By the end of the campaign she did not feel so isolated. She had also grown resigned to her husband's womanizing antics. A beautiful young woman came on board as FDR's secretary. In short time, Marguerite "Missy" LeHand became enough of an insider that she stayed with the Roosevelts in Hyde Park.

The election was a landslide victory for the Republicans. FDR, along with the majority of the Democratic candidates, was defeated. He seemed to take the loss in stride, but inside he worried. He was 38 years old, and his political future was uncertain. He created a law partnership with friends, a Wall Street firm specializing in wills and estates. FDR and Eleanor headed back to New York, he to try to make money and Eleanor to focus on an issue that had become important to her: women.

Women were granted the right to vote in 1920. All of a sudden, 26 million women could vote. Through her work on social-justice issues, Eleanor had been fully aware of the barriers women faced, but she only supported suffrage for women after her husband had endorsed it. By 1921, though, Eleanor was involved in every aspect of the women's political movement. Through her involvement, Eleanor began to make close friends.

POLIO STRIKES

In 1921, Franklin was torn between his desire to help Eleanor in her activities and having a wife who was making

In late July 1921, Franklin Roosevelt *(far left)* visited a Boy Scout camp at Lake Kanohwahke in New York. This is the last known picture of Roosevelt walking unassisted. Two weeks later, he contracted polio.

headlines. His law practice was hardly inspiring, and he started to drink more and attend parties more. At one family function, he acted out of control from alcohol, and another time, in June 1921, he could not get out of bed because of a hangover. Eleanor was furious and let him know it.

He remained in New York the following week while she moved their kids to Campobello, where soon all 18 bedrooms were filled with family and visitors. Franklin had been worried that his political career would never get off the ground again. He was tired when he left to go to Campobello on a yacht that a friend was lending him. The weather was stormy, but Franklin arrived safely with a group of friends who wanted to be entertained. After days of jogging and swimming and nonstop activities, Franklin came home one afternoon complaining of chills. He did not have supper and went to bed early. The next day, he had a fever and a great deal of pain in his back and legs. At first, the doctor thought he had a blood clot, and massages were recommended. Eleanor stepped in to care for him, working around the clock. For three weeks he did not improve, and in fact his condition worsened. Specialists were brought in, and all were baffled. Finally, at the end of August, a Boston specialist said that he had the dreaded disease polio. It was terrifying news. Twenty-five percent of people who caught polio died of it within the first two weeks. Those who survived often suffered from paralysis the rest of their lives.

Eleanor and Franklin decided to present a cheerful front when Franklin's mother returned from Europe. Louis Howe made a big effort to keep information about his boss's illness out of the press. In September, Franklin was secretly moved to a hospital in New York City, where he remained until mid-December. When he was allowed to leave, Eleanor moved a nurse into their home in Manhattan, and Louis Howe also moved in. Many friends and associates were certain Franklin's political career was over. But they did not know Eleanor Roosevelt.

Reinventing
Eleanor

Franklin Roosevelt's future, Eleanor Roosevelt fervently believed, depended on her husband maintaining a positive attitude. With that in mind, she worked every minute in his behalf, keeping him informed of what was going on politically. Her mother-in-law took the opposite approach, believing that his recovery depended on his retirement from public life. Sara thought she could do with Franklin as she had done with his father, who had had recurring heart ailments: She would take care of him, and he could pursue his hobbies.

Eleanor knew that her husband's soul would be destroyed if that happened to him. For the first time in her life, she openly confronted her mother-in-law. She was now the voice for his inner needs and feelings. Eleanor admitted later that it was the most trying winter of her life. Not only was she worried about her husband, but her mother-in-law had worked to turn Eleanor's daughter, Anna, against her. Eleanor ended up behaving much as her own mother had behaved with her, becoming cold and distant and refusing to share her worries with her teenage daughter. One afternoon, while reading to Johnny and Franklin Jr.—who were only five and seven—Eleanor broke down in tears and could not stop crying. Her children, who had never seen their mother express such emotions, fled the room. They were beginning to sense the enormity of the situation.

FDR refused to accept the doctors' verdict that he would never walk again. No one would ever know how he felt, not his mother nor his wife, as he never was able to express his despair around them. After 1922, Franklin spent most of his time fishing and recuperating in Florida. He bought a houseboat and filled his days with aimless fun. The ever-devoted "Missy" LeHand joined him there. Historian Doris Kearns Goodwin said in an interview, "Missy had started working for Franklin when she was 20 years old in 1920, and I think fell in love with him and never stopped loving him all the rest of her life."[1] She learned to fish and was by his side constantly.

Eleanor and Franklin's son James said, "These were the lonely years. We had no tangible father, no father whom we could touch and talk to, only a cheery letter-writer."[2] Eleanor, in her newfound wisdom, understood that her husband would be the one who would be transformed by his paralysis. She said, "He had to think out the fundamentals of living and learn the greatest of all lessons—infinite patience and never-ending persistence."[3]

His long illness became another turning point for Eleanor as she engaged in far more activities than she had in the past. Politics became an increasingly important part of her life. She joined the Women's Trade Union League in 1922 and the Women's Division of the New York Democratic Party in 1923. They were reformist organizations made up of feminists dedicated to the establishment of a minimum wage, the protection of laborers, and the end of child labor. Louis Howe, now a devoted friend of Eleanor's, too, convinced her that it would be up to her to keep Franklin's name alive in political circles. He monitored her speeches to help her improve. She claimed to be speaking in behalf of her husband, but she was developing her own ideas. Eleanor had decided that she wanted to help others and that she was good at it. She developed a keen interest in child labor, public housing, and unemployment insurance, becoming a voice for those who had none.

Franklin invited her to come down to Florida often, but she did not like the people who were around him. She knew that "Missy" LeHand was with him and that there was no room for her. Historian David McCullough said, "She had accepted that she and her husband were bound together by politics, respect, and real affection, but they led separate lives."[4]

Although women had won the right to vote, it was still hard to persuade the men who ran party politics to listen to them. As elections drew closer in 1924, Eleanor battled with New York City political boss Charles Murphy to allow women to choose the women delegates to the Democratic Party's state convention. He insisted on selecting them, and Eleanor threatened to go to the press. He persisted, and she did what she said she would. She was quoted as saying, "We [women] will be enormously strengthened if we can show that we are willing to fight to the very last ditch for what we believe in."[5] Murphy gave in, and Eleanor was thrilled to have won her first political fight.

That same year Franklin was invited to the Democratic National Convention, but he was too weak to do anything but make a speech. He rejected all talk of his running for

Eleanor Roosevelt is shown at the Democratic State Convention, held in April 1924 in Albany, New York. She tangled with a prominent political boss, who had wanted to appoint all the women delegates to the convention. In the end, Eleanor prevailed, winning her first political victory.

governor of New York. He declared that he would not seek public office until he could walk without crutches. With that in mind, he shifted his Southern residence to Warm Springs, Georgia, where he had heard of steaming mineral water that had healing powers.

Once a vacation resort, the buildings at Warm Springs were rundown, and Franklin dreamed of restoring them into a modern rehabilitation center. Eleanor worried that his new passion would take him away from politics. He exploded at her and told her she either supported him or she didn't. She did. He invested two-thirds of his personal fortune and created the first modern treatment center for people with polio. Here, Franklin was an ordinary person, one of the many hoping to be healed. He brought in black-smiths who designed braces, and he invented a muscle-testing technique that is still in use today. He designed a car that he could manage without his legs. Franklin drove around Georgia, meeting the people, and they came to love him. He struggled daily to learn to walk again. He hated crutches, for he thought they inspired pity.

NEW FRIENDS

Eleanor and Franklin were not together often. They kept up with each other's whereabouts and agreed to keep certain things from FDR's mother. Eleanor spent a great deal of time with her new friends, especially Nancy Cook and Marion Dickerman, who lived in Greenwich Village. Cook was an organizer in the Democratic Party, and Dickerman was a teacher and the first woman to run for the New York State Legislature. Dickerman became head of the private Todhunter School in New York, and Eleanor started to teach literature and history there three days a week. In 1925, Franklin drew up a lease giving Cook, Dickerman, and Eleanor life interest in a property two miles from the Roosevelt manor of Springwood. He arranged for the construction of a small stone house, and they shared the building costs. Val-Kill, named after Fallkill Creek, which ran beside the house, became a permanent home for Cook and Dickerman and a retreat for Eleanor. The following year, the women built a larger building on the property in which they established a furniture-making shop with the

VAL-KILL

Alhough Eleanor Roosevelt was raised in a prestigious family and married into an illustrious family, she never had her own house. She and her husband lived in homes provided by his mother. In the mid-1920s, Eleanor moved into a modest and simple field-stone Dutch colonial cottage built on property two miles from Springwood, Sara Roosevelt's impressive house situated on a hill overlooking the Hudson River. The home at Val-Kill was shared by her two close friends, Nancy Cook and Marion Dickerman. Next door, they built a factory where reproductions of early American furniture were manufactured. After the business closed in 1936, Eleanor Roosevelt converted the building into a home for herself alone.

The two houses today are part of the Eleanor Roosevelt National Historic Site. A long driveway leads to the two houses. The second house, Val-Kill Cottage, looks today much as it did when Eleanor was alive. It is lovely in its simplicity. An oval dining room table is set with the china she used. She slept on a twin bed with a chenille bedspread. Dozens of family photos surround the bed, along with pictures of Nikita Khrushchev, Charles DeGaulle, and Winston Churchill.

goal of creating jobs for rural workers. Eleanor grew to love hiking, and lost her fear of mountain climbing. She loved to swim and ride and drive fast.

The three women bought the Todhunter School for Girls in 1926. Eleanor could not believe how much she enjoyed her new life. She became director of the Bureau of Women's Activities for the Democratic Party, and her

Val-Kill was the house Eleanor retired to after her husband died. It was here where she felt most like her true self. She could write and restore her energy. She attended a Hyde Park church wearing cotton dresses and tennis shoes. She shopped at road-side stands and did a little gardening.

In the small stucco cottage is a study where Eleanor and her secretary and friend, Malvina "Tommy" Thompson, worked each day answering letters. Eleanor liked to sleep on the screened-in, wood-paneled porch. She spent her last years at Val-Kill in simple solitude, enjoying the visits of old political allies, family members, and friends.

After Eleanor died, the property was sold, and the house was divided into little apartments. In 1977, it was purchased by a preservationist group. Today, the converted factory is a shrine maintained by the National Park Service and the cottage is used by a private group that keeps her ideals alive. Both Eleanor and Franklin are buried in the rose garden at Franklin's mother's home, Springwood. Their memorial is a simple rectangular white stone carved with their names and the dates of their births and deaths.

articles on every subject—from parenting to foreign policy—were published in various women's magazines. Not only had she found a way to have more freedom, but she was earning thousands of dollars of her own.

BACK TO POLITICS

After five years, Franklin had developed a technique that looked like walking. He relied on his sons, who did exercises to make their arms strong. Their father would lean on one of them, switching his weight from the son's arm onto the cane he now carried. He instructed his sons to make it look easy. His newfound way of maneuvering his body was dangerous, as it was extremely unstable, but it worked politically. No one would vote for a man who looked weak.

Eleanor had been right all along. Her husband belonged in politics. When Alfred E. Smith, the four-term New York governor who was running for president in 1928, asked Franklin to run for governor of New York, he was ready. Later Smith was asked why he had put Roosevelt, a potential rival, back in the political spotlight. Smith replied that he thought Roosevelt would be dead within a year. FDR won the election, and the family moved back to Albany, where Eleanor divided her time between assisting her husband and participating in her own activities. Part of her new role was to act as Franklin's eyes and ears. It was during this period that their partnership based on respect and similar goals became strong, and lasting.

THE GREAT DEPRESSION

The stock market crashed on October 24, 1929. Soon, 14 million people—a third of the workforce—would be out of jobs. Republican President Herbert Hoover fell into despair along with the rest of the nation, believing the government could not turn the economy around. The country was in the midst of the Great Depression. FDR, however, was making a name for himself by introducing bold new ideas in New York. He insisted that it was the duty of the government to do something about the condition of the people.

As governor, he created the Temporary Emergency Relief Administration, which provided state-funded jobs to the unemployed, lent money to businesses in trouble, and gave pensions to the elderly. Because of his policies, FDR was reelected governor in 1930 by the largest margin ever in the state. He was back in the national spotlight and was seen as the front-runner to win the Democratic nomination to run for president in 1932.

That year, FDR was invited to a dinner at the White House for governors. The White House butler at the time, Alonzo Fields, told how FDR arrived at the dinner, with a cane in his hand and dragging his legs from his hips while

IN HER OWN WORDS

One of Franklin D. Roosevelt's most famous quotations, from his 1932 inaugural address, has to do with "fear." Eleanor Roosevelt also had eloquent words on that subject. In *You Learn by Living: Eleven Keys for a More Fulfilling Life*, Eleanor Roosevelt's 1960 book, she wrote:

> Courage is more exhilarating than fear and in the long run it is easier. We do not have to become heroes overnight. Just a step at a time, meeting each thing that comes up, seeing it is not as dreadful as it appeared, discovering we have the strength to stare it down.

Franklin Roosevelt showed off one of the many congratulatory telegrams he received after winning the presidential election in November 1932. Despite the smile on her face, Eleanor Roosevelt was not looking forward to becoming the first lady. She feared she would lose much of the political independence she had gained.

leaning on a bodyguard's arm. He fell into his seat. People at the table were stunned. On July 1, 1932, he was named the Democratic nominee for the president of the United States. The people knew the story of how he had worked his way back, and it was a symbol to them of a victory they longed for. His wonderful smile and boundless confidence was like the answer to a prayer.

It was Louis Howe who told Eleanor that her husband was going to run for president in 1932. The thought of giving up her own political life was almost more than Eleanor could bear. She was happy for her husband, but, she said, "For myself I was deeply troubled. This meant the end of any personal life of my own."[6]

Franklin D. Roosevelt was elected, but the months before his inauguration were the worst the country had ever experienced. Five thousand banks closed. The economy had completely collapsed. Historian David McCullough, who narrated a PBS program called *The Presidents*, said, "On March 4, 1933, a man who could not walk would begin to lead the crippled country."[7]

During his inaugural address, FDR spoke the line that would reverberate for decades. He said, "Let me assert my firm belief that the only thing we have to fear is fear itself—nameless, unreasoning, unjustified terror."[8] In the past, presidents had received as few as 200 letters in a week. After his address to the nation, FDR received nearly half a million. In one day, he had established himself as the leader the country had been seeking. It was time now for Eleanor Roosevelt to overcome her dread in becoming the first lady and figure out how to adapt to her new role.

Revolutionizing the Role of the First Lady

Moving into the White House was a difficult adjustment for Eleanor Roosevelt. Not only was she at loose ends as to how to conduct her life, but she felt her family was falling apart. Her daughter, Anna, was getting a divorce and moved into the White House with her two children. Her son Elliott was leaving his wife. Her husband had asked her to give up teaching at Todhunter School. There was nothing to hang onto.

It was at this extremely vulnerable time that she invited newspaper reporter Lorena Hickok, whom she had gotten to know on the campaign trail, into her life as her closest friend and confidante. "Hick" became devoted to Eleanor, and there have been many rumors over the years that she and Eleanor were in love, but there has never been proof of a romantic relationship. The two women became inseparable for several years. Eleanor's grandson Franklin III said in an interview that "these were two needy people and they discovered that they could fulfill each other's needs."[1] No one had ever been so devoted to Eleanor. Through the friendship, Franklin Roosevelt III added, "She [Eleanor] developed an emotional capacity which had not always been there."[2]

"Hick" helped her friend define her role as first lady and taught her how to deal with the press. She encouraged Eleanor to hold press conferences for women reporters only, which forced newspapers to hire more women. Eleanor's first news conference was held two days after her husband's inauguration. Eventually, she would hold nearly 350 of them. Hickok also suggested that Eleanor write a column for the newspapers, which Eleanor started to do in 1936. It was called "My Day." Hickok accompanied Eleanor on some of her trips, including one to San Juan, Puerto Rico, in 1934. There, they visited the city's slums in an effort to show the American people what the poverty in Puerto Rico was like. The response to their trip was positive.

THE NEW DEAL

During a speech in his campaign, Franklin Roosevelt had promised what he called "a new deal for the forgotten man."[3] From this emerged the New Deal, the series of programs that FDR initiated as president. The goal of the New Deal was to bring about the recovery of the economy, give work to the unemployed, and reform business and finance practices.

Immediately after taking office, the president aimed his first initiatives at short-term recovery. He pledged billions to save farms and homes from foreclosure, and he guaranteed the savings of millions. The administration implemented banking-reform laws, emergency-relief programs, work-relief

As first lady, Eleanor Roosevelt *(in the white hat)* toured a street in San Juan, Puerto Rico, in 1934 to see the living conditions there. With her was her close friend and confidante, Lorena Hickok *(second to the right from Roosevelt)*, who had been a newspaper reporter.

programs, agricultural programs, and industrial reform. By the time FDR had served 100 days, he had signed 15 major bills into law. Among the agencies created were the Farm Security Administration, the Rural Electrification Administration, the Public Works Administration, the National Recovery Administration, and the Subsistence Homesteads Program. It was the first time the U.S. government had ever made an attempt to directly help citizens who had suffered financial hardship.

During the first year of her husband's term, Eleanor Roosevelt traveled across the country, giving speeches, meeting people, and witnessing the devastation of the Depression. She logged some 40,000 miles (64,000 kilometers). Eleanor reported all she saw and heard back to FDR, often convincing him of her views.

Sometimes, Eleanor's popularity ratings were even higher than her husband's. She revolutionized the role of first lady. She spoke for blacks, women, factory workers, and tenant farmers. She started a practice of writing memos to FDR about issues that he needed to address, writing so many that he finally had to tell her to keep it to three per night. Their grandson Curtis Roosevelt said in a PBS interview:

> What they had together—our grandmother and grandfather—was what I call a creative tension. They both basically believed in the same things, but they had different roles to play. . . . He had to work with the Congress. . . . She was able to influence issues and he was delighted, but he could also disown her and did with the press. He would say, "Well, you know my missus. I don't dictate what she says," . . . which was very, very convenient—convenient for him to, through her, sense how far he could go.[4]

Eleanor Roosevelt influenced policy in ways both large and small. One of her more informal methods was her famous Sunday egg scrambles. Each Sunday, she invited people from all walks of life to a family dinner of scrambled eggs. There, they would be able to talk casually with the president about what was important to them. FDR was then able to develop New Deal policy based on the living realities of the people. Eleanor said at one point, "I'm the agitator; he's the politician."[5] A speechwriter for the president said that she was "the keeper and constant spokesman for her husband's conscience."[6]

One of the larger ways in which Eleanor exerted her influence was with a project in the Subsistence Homesteads Program, which sought to reduce rural poverty by building planned communities where people would farm small plots or work at nearby factories. During one of her trips, Eleanor Roosevelt visited the poor mining community of Scott's Run, West Virginia. She thought Scott's Run was an ideal candidate for the Subsistence Homesteads Program. In 1933, families in the area began to build a housing community called Arthurdale. Eleanor was determined to make it work. She went there once a month. She got to know the people and inquired after their families. Ultimately, though, the experiment failed in the 1940s— the residents could not grow enough to feed themselves, and businesses could not get established. Eleanor learned the limits of power and influence.

Still, a first lady had never before taken such an active interest in politics. Sometimes she was referred to in print as the co-president. Opinion differs on just how influential she was with her husband, but no one will argue that the New Deal had her stamp on it. American thought was changed forever by what came to be referred to as "the Roosevelt Way." The belief that held firm for so long—that a person should make it on his or her own—was gone. Eleanor Roosevelt said it best in 1936: "We should strive to give every individual a chance for a decent and secure existence; and in evolving our social patterns we are trying to give both hope for better things in the future, and freedom from want in the present."[7]

CHAMPION OF CIVIL RIGHTS

The community she had grown up in did not include African Americans, even as servants. In an essay titled,

"Some of My Best Friends Are Negro," she explained that she learned about African Americans by listening to her great-aunt Mrs. James King Gracie, who had been born and raised on a Georgia plantation. She read to Eleanor and her siblings from Brer Rabbit books. Eleanor was 15 and in Europe when she met a black person for the first time. She was 49 years old when she began to inspect New Deal programs in the South and discovered the shocking level of discrimination against blacks. She immediately became an outspoken champion of civil rights. Through her barrage of memos and explanation, FDR signed a series of executive orders barring discrimination in the administration of various New Deal agencies. According to historian Doris Kearns Goodwin, this was the beginning of Eleanor's independent legacy.

OPPOSITION TO THE NEW DEAL

Republicans, including many friends of the Roosevelt family and alumni from Groton School and Harvard College, criticized the new government as being too big and faulted FDR for meddling with free enterprise. They had understood that the programs established to help the people were temporary. When Franklin Roosevelt began to regulate the stock exchange and the banks, they grew angrier. In 1935, a day New Dealers would come to refer to as Black Monday, the Supreme Court declared that the National Recovery Act and other laws were unconstitutional. In short, the court set out to dismantle everything Roosevelt had achieved. FDR was unstoppable, though. He created the WPA, or Works Progress Administration, which created jobs for out-of-work people. He offered the Social Security Act to assist millions, claiming that the poor had rights, too. The wealthy accused him of pitting class against class.

When Franklin was up for a second term in 1936, his opponent, Alf Landon, attacked his New Deal policies and criticized Eleanor for being a nontraditional first lady. There was no question that FDR had made many enemies along the way, especially those among his class who felt betrayed. They despised the unions that organized around labor and the higher taxes imposed on them. Franklin Roosevelt had shifted the balance of power in the United States. On the other hand, the New Deal had given jobs to six million people, and corporate profits were rising. African Americans, who had traditionally voted Republican, switched parties. Eleanor, too, was both loved and hated, coming under attack for her strong support of the New Deal programs and for the sympathies she displayed for black Americans. Despite the criticism against the Roosevelts, though, Franklin Roosevelt won a landslide victory in the 1936 presidential election.

A FRUSTRATING SECOND TERM

The euphoria was not to last. Roosevelt lost some of his power by trying to rein in the Supreme Court, which had overturned several of the president's New Deal programs. Roosevelt proposed a bill to allow him to appoint extra justices to the Supreme Court so that he could outnumber his opponents. His efforts failed. The stock market crashed again, and millions remained out of work. But what was most disturbing were the sounds of war that could be heard in the distance. Adolf Hitler had seized control in Germany, the Italian dictator Benito Mussolini had invaded Ethiopia, and Japan had started a war with China.

The United States had become isolationist, meaning it kept to itself, far removed from the problems of other countries. The members of Congress held a firm line on remaining neutral in the world's conflicts. Hitler knew this, and Roosevelt knew that he knew. It was terribly frustrating. Every time the president attempted to play a role on the world stage, those who hated Roosevelt claimed that he was trying to get the country into war. In March 1938, German troops occupied Austria, followed by Czechoslovakia, with no one calling Hitler's bluff. Roosevelt felt that war was inevitable, but his hands were tied by Congress. Roosevelt's second term had not gone as well as his first. He did not have Congress in his pocket, millions remained without work, and Europe was on the brink of war.

With his government at a stalemate, he did something never done before. He invited the king and queen of England to the United States. It was a brilliant idea, for Americans were enchanted by the couple. Three months after they returned to England, the British were at war with Hitler. Their royal couple's visit to the United States had won many over to FDR's way of thinking.

As opposed as the American people were to war, FDR knew that it was only a matter of time. He had served two terms and was prepared to leave office. No president had ever served more than two terms. But as more people began to see war on the horizon, many begged him to run again.

DID YOU KNOW?

Eleanor Roosevelt befriended Amelia Earhart, who was 13 years younger. In 1932, Earhart invited Roosevelt to take a flight over the nation's capital, and she accepted. Earhart, to mark the occasion, wore an evening gown while flying the plane. They also went on a joyride around the White House grounds in a race car. Roosevelt wanted to learn how to fly, and Earhart agreed to teach her. Roosevelt even got her student permit, but before the lessons could begin, Earhart left on her journey to become the first woman to fly around the world. During her trip, on July 2, 1937, Earhart's plane disappeared between New Guinea and Howland Island in the Pacific Ocean.

After receiving a standing ovation at the 1940 Democratic National Convention in Chicago, Eleanor Roosevelt acknowledged the crowd. Eleanor, who had spoken in defense of her husband's vice presidential pick, was the first wife of a president to address a national political convention.

He was torn, as he had started to grow tired and he wanted to go home. On the other hand, he wanted to have a hand in what was going on in the world. The man running against him, Wendell Willkie, campaigned against both Roosevelts. A slogan pin that he handed out said, "I don't want Eleanor either."[8]

Eleanor was not to be deterred. She had faced enough criticism by this time that she had learned to stand her ground. On July 17, 1940, delegates to the Democratic National Convention had nominated FDR to serve a third term. The delegates, however, threatened to revolt when he said he wanted Henry Wallace, a controversial figure, as his running mate. He called Eleanor, who was at Val-Kill, and asked her to go to the convention in Chicago. The next day, she stood before the delegates, and the hall grew quiet. She explained that this was no ordinary time. And then she said, "No man who is a candidate or who is president can carry this situation alone. This is only carried by a united people who love their country and who will live for it to the fullest of their ability, with a determination to bring the world to a safer and happier condition."[9] The people broke into wild applause. Some thought a miracle had taken place. Eleanor beamed at her audience. It was the first time in history that the wife of a presidential nominee had addressed a major political convention.

She considered their third term in the White House a huge sacrifice, but as always, she began to think how her energy and intelligence could best be used.

The War Years

In the spring of 1940, Adolf Hitler invaded Denmark, Norway, Holland, and Belgium, then focused on France. France fell within days. In August, Germany began an assault on Britain. President Franklin D. Roosevelt desperately wanted to help when the British prime minister sought his assistance. Congress had prohibited the president from sending weapons to the British unless they paid in cash, but Britain had no money. Roosevelt, though, figured out a way to get around this problem. He created the Lend-Lease Act, which allowed the United States to lend war supplies to the British. Americans thought it was a good compromise.

In the meantime, FDR created the Office of Civilian Defense (OCD) with the goal of enlisting men and women as defense volunteers. Eleanor Roosevelt was thrilled, thinking more along domestic lines. Why couldn't the agency also help people socially and economically? When Mayor Fiorello La Guardia of New York was put in charge, Eleanor was pleased. As she worked with him, though, she thought that he had a narrow vision. He offered her a job as the assistant director of the OCD. She accepted—never before had a first lady held a government job. She loved the work, but the criticism did not stop. Congressmen in the House of Representatives rose from their seats one after another to attack her. Eleanor had come to understand long before "that a woman who insisted on her right to self-identity, a woman with power or the appearance of power was bound to elicit people's rage and contempt."[1] After five months, feeling that her role was no longer helpful to the OCD, she resigned.

ATTACK ON PEARL HARBOR

By mid-1941, the Nazis had sunk more than 1,500 British ships. FDR was ready to go to war, even if he had to do it in secret. Roosevelt had issued covert orders to allow the U.S. Navy to escort British convoys and sink German submarines if necessary. In September, the United States destroyer Greer was attacked by a German submarine. Even then, Roosevelt did not ask Congress for a declaration of war, but he did use the incident to justify an undeclared war in the Atlantic Ocean.

In the fall, FDR's mother, Sara, died. In that same year, all four of the Roosevelts' sons were called to active duty. Eleanor was no different from any other woman in the United States who was sending her child or spouse off to serve in the military as war loomed.

On December 7, 1941, Japanese bombers attacked the American naval fleet at Pearl Harbor, killing nearly 2,500 sailors and civilians. President Roosevelt could

First Lady Eleanor Roosevelt and Mayor Fiorello La Guardia of New York prepared to board a plane for Los Angeles to organize defense activities on the West Coast. La Guardia was director of the Office of Civilian Defense, and Roosevelt was the assistant director.

not believe that the Navy had been caught unaware. He felt disgraced. In telling the country about the attack, he held back, never acknowledging that the entire Pacific fleet had been devastated. In her radio address that night, Eleanor said, "For months now the knowledge that something of this kind might happen has been hanging over our heads. . . . That is all over now, and there is no more uncertainty. We know what we have to face, and we know we are ready to face it. . . . We are the free and unconquerable people of the U.S.A."[2]

The United States declared war on Japan. Four days later, Hitler declared war on the United States. It was one disaster after another after that. The Japanese swept through Southeast Asia, and the Germans advanced into Russia. Just two weeks after Pearl Harbor, Prime Minister Winston Churchill of Great Britain came to the White House to talk military strategy with the president. The main decision—which country to fight first, Germany or Japan? After a month of discussions, Churchill and Roosevelt had decided to fight the Germans first, though the Allies were still too weak to invade Europe. The American military needed to be built up. To increase weapons production, FDR had private companies start to make arms. He set war-production goals—60,000 planes in 1942, 125,000 planes the following year. By November 1942, Roosevelt was able to send 80,000 U.S. troops to fight Hitler's men in North Africa. Two months later, he joined them there and met with Churchill at Casablanca, Morocco.

THE FIRST LADY'S ACTIONS

Eleanor was passionate about three issues during the war years: refugees, soldiers' concerns, and homefront issues, which included keeping the New Deal alive. Even before the United States entered the war, Eleanor had worked to change strict U.S. immigration laws to allow refugees from

Germany to come to the United States. She worked with the Emergency Rescue Committee, the U.S. Committee for the Care of European Children, and the Children's

ELEANOR AND CIVIL RIGHTS

Eleanor Roosevelt began to focus on racial discrimination after she moved into the White House in 1933. She believed in equal opportunity for all, but initially she accepted segregation. She stirred up a hornets' nest in the White House with her insistence that FDR support an anti-lynching bill in 1934. He was too worried about alienating the Southern senators to support it. When Eleanor went to an art exhibit called *A Commentary on Lynching*, Southern critics seized the opportunity to criticize her husband.

A woman named Mary McLeod Bethune, whom Eleanor Roosevelt had met in 1927, helped her understand the problems facing black Americans. Eleanor and Bethune became good friends. Eleanor also read black author Richard Wright, who helped to shape her opinion.

Eleanor Roosevelt invited black singer Marian Anderson to perform at the White House in 1936. In 1938, she invited her to perform for the visit of the British monarchs the following spring. She also planned to present the Spingarn Medal to the singer at the NAACP's convention that year. Members of the Daughters of the American Revolution (DAR) refused to allow Anderson to sing at Constitution Hall. In her "My Day" column, Eleanor announced her resignation from the DAR on February 27, 1939. The column appeared in 400 newspapers and became a national issue. The first lady did not stop there. She arranged for Anderson to sing at the Lincoln Memorial in Washington. She pressured radio stations to cover the

Crusade for Children. She tried to help individuals, but there was little she could do to help the hundreds who petitioned her to come to the United States. In 1939,

event live and urged the NAACP to use the concert as a fund-raiser.

During World War II, she said repeatedly that democracy could not exist in the United States if there was no democracy for blacks. She visited black soldiers, against intense opposition. She was blamed for race riots that broke out in Detroit in 1943. She was decades ahead of her time.

Civil-rights leader Vernon Jarrett said that, as much as Eleanor Roosevelt contributed to the African-American cause, it would be wrong to say that she was "the cause of the Negro movements of that time, the civil rights movements. This came from the black people themselves," he said.* He saw Eleanor as a woman who "did not object to the continual discovery of self, of what she was about."** And in his mind, "the more she discovered herself, the more she became sensitized to what was happening to black people."***

---

*American Experience: Eleanor Roosevelt, Vernon Jarrett on Eleanor's Commitment to African Americans. Transcript available online at http://www.pbs.org/wgbh/amex/eleanor/filmmore/reference/interview/jarrett07.html.

**American Experience, Eleanor Roosevelt, Vernon Jarrett on: Being African American. http://www.pbs.org/wgbh/amex/eleanor/filmmore/reference/interview/jarretto1.html.

***Vernon Jarrett on Eleanor's Commitment to African Americans.

despite her lobbying, Congress refused to pass a bill that would have allowed 10,000 Jewish children above the usual German quota to enter the United States. It was an uphill battle all the way. Finally, President Roosevelt created the War Refugee Board to help civil victims of the Nazis, but it was established late in the war, in January 1944.

Eleanor Roosevelt could see America's own failings during World War II, and it was painful. As much as Americans despised Hitler and what he stood for, in America a black soldier in uniform had to be careful. She continued as a voice for civil rights, insisting that the United States could not fight racism abroad while tolerating it at home. She said, "The basic fact of segregation, which warps and twists the lives of our Negro population, [is] itself discriminatory."[3] Her efforts brought more opportunities for blacks in the factories and in the armed forces overseas.

SUPPORT OF WOMEN

Women entered the workforce in droves, filling the vacant jobs left by the men who had gone off to war. A woman working for a paycheck was a new concept. Eleanor saw it as an opportunity for women to become independent by earning their own money. She encouraged women to work in the factories, where they could learn a skill, and she threw out subtle cautions about marrying too young. She played a big role in getting the government to set aside funds for child-care centers.

In her book titled *The Home Front and Beyond: American Women in the 1940s*, Susan M. Hartmann believed that the move by women into the public realm represented the most substantial change of the 1940s, but the change was not uniform. Gender roles in the United States were restructured because so many men had gone to war, but it was to be temporary. Through propaganda, women understood that what they were doing was to bring home their men and help make the world safe for children. Eleanor fought against such ideas, saying that everyone who wanted to work should have that right. She was furious when the child-care centers were closed after the war.

However, the opportunities afforded women during the war years altered their behavior and beliefs about their proper place. They laid the foundation for "an awakened womanhood in the 1960s," according to Hartmann.[4]

A tide of prejudice arose against Japanese Americans after Pearl Harbor was attacked. There was widespread panic. Eleanor allowed herself to be photographed with American-born Japanese. She also spoke in public about the ugly prejudice, but her tolerance angered many Americans. President Roosevelt, after great persuasion from the military and West Coast officials, signed Executive Order 9066 in February 1942. People of Japanese descent were forced from their homes and were transported to internment camps that had been built on racetracks and athletic fields on the West Coast. About 120,000 people of Japanese ethnicity were held at the camps during World War II. Eleanor Roosevelt had spoken privately to her husband many times against the executive order, but she failed to persuade him not to issue it.

ELEANOR ABROAD

Eleanor poured her seemingly boundless energy into traveling the world to visit soldiers, operating under the code name "Rover," given to her by the FBI. She went to the South Pacific, traveling more than 23,000 miles (37,000 kilometers). She was given the nickname "Everywhere Eleanor," for no one knew where she might turn up. Another named bestowed on her was "Public Energy Number One." One time, she entered a tent and bumped into two soldiers who were not wearing their trousers. She calmly sat down and chatted with them. Admiral William Halsey,

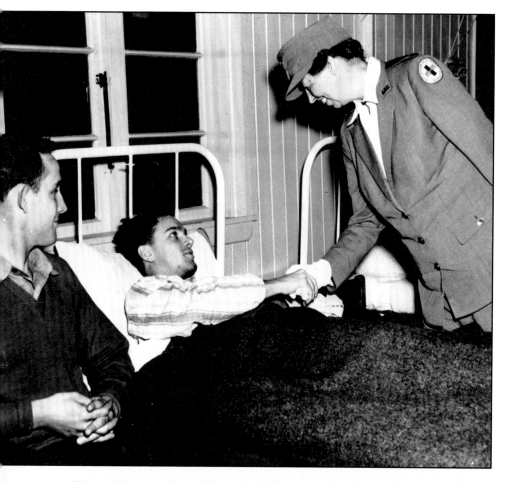

Eleanor Roosevelt shook hands with injured soldier Theodore Truesdell in September 1943 on her tour of the South Pacific during World War II. "She alone accomplished more good than any other person who passed through my area," said Admiral William Halsey, commander of the Pacific fleet.

commander of the Pacific fleet, had opposed her visit to his men, but he later changed his mind. He said, "She saw patients who were grievously wounded. I marveled most at their (patients') expressions as she leaned over them. . . . She alone accomplished more good than any other person who passed through my area."[5]

On June 6, 1944, Americans streamed into the streets as church bells and school bells rang across the nation. Allied forces had landed on the beaches of Normandy, France, in their attempt to liberate Europe. Eleanor wrote that she "lived suspended in space, waiting for news of the invasion, dreading the inevitable and horrible loss of life, yet wishing it success. It was a success, but at a great cost of lives."[6] Three weeks after the invasion, she said that "all emotion is drained away."[7]

A FOURTH TERM

With the United States still fighting World War II, FDR decided to run for a fourth term. He was 62 years old and had been president for 11 years. Eleanor believed that his remaining in office would be good for the country, although the idea of being in the White House for four more years depressed her. FDR was weaker than when he had started his presidency, but Eleanor believed strongly that an iron will could conquer illness. This time Franklin was running against Thomas E. Dewey. Eleanor was too busy traveling the world as a goodwill ambassador, and Franklin was too ill and busy running the country to campaign. When it started to look as if Franklin might lose, both became political whirlwinds once again. When asked how Franklin managed to find the strength, a campaign worker answered, "It was largely due to the determination of Mrs. Roosevelt."[8] President Roosevelt was reelected again on November 7, 1944.

In February 1945, Joseph Stalin of the Soviet Union, Winston Churchill of Great Britain, and Franklin Roosevelt met in secret at Yalta, a Russian resort on the Black Sea, to discuss peace and many unresolved issues surrounding the war. Eleanor desperately wanted to go, but FDR took their daughter, Anna, instead. He was beginning to depend more and more on Anna. After returning from Yalta, the president addressed Congress. Roosevelt had been in poor health for several months, and for the first time, he gave his speech sitting down.

DEATH OF A GIANT

Two months later, on April 12, 1945, Franklin Delano Roosevelt died in Warm Springs, Georgia. Eleanor went there immediately. She learned an unbearable truth after she arrived. Lucy Mercer, now widowed, had been with the president when he died. She had taken an artist to paint FDR's portrait and had been there for three days. With Anna's help, she had been making secret visits for the past year to the White House and to Warm Springs to be with the man she had never stopped loving. Eleanor held her head high, but it would take a long time to get over Anna's betrayal.

The day of her husband's death, Eleanor stood with Vice President Harry Truman as he was sworn in as president. Then she joined those who were taking the president's body to Washington. He was buried at the family estate, Springwood, in Hyde Park. Eleanor watched as men shoveled dirt into his grave. Later she said, "One cannot say good-bye to people whom they have loved . . . without deep emotion, but at last even that was over. I was now on my own."[9]

Her voice sounds cold in that statement. Doris Kearns Goodwin, in her book *No Ordinary Time: Franklin and Eleanor Roosevelt: The Home Front in World War II*, tells in the final pages of her book how Franklin, "broken in health and isolated as much by the history of his marriage as by the burdens of office," appears terribly lonely, as does Eleanor.[10] According to their son Elliott, FDR began to look forward to the day when he would no longer be president. "I think Mother and I might be able to get together now and do some things together, take some trips maybe, learn to know each other again," he told his son.[11]

But it was not a time for regret. Kearns wrote of Eleanor, "Had she been given the choice between supplying the relaxation for her husband that Lucy was providing or summoning her powers to effect a change in the lives of Negro Americans, she would undoubtedly have chosen the latter."[12]

The war was about to be over, too. Germany surrendered to the Allies in May 1945, and the Japanese surrendered in August after the United States dropped atomic bombs on the Japanese cities of Hiroshima and Nagasaki. Eleanor did not feel like celebrating. And no wonder—406,000 Americans had died in the war. She wrote to Anna, "I miss Pa's voice, and the words he would have spoken."[13]

First Lady
of the World

When asked about her plans after Franklin Roosevelt's death, Eleanor Roosevelt answered: "The story is over."[1] Little did she know in that moment that her personal story was about to begin. Days after FDR's death, Eleanor moved back to her beloved Val-Kill, near Hyde Park, where she could reflect. She was 60 years old and knew that she "did not want to run an elaborate household again, did not want to cease being useful in some way, and did not want to feel old."[2]

Some suggested that Eleanor should run for the U.S. Senate, but she said no. She thought that her skills and her strengths could be put to better use somewhere else. She and FDR, in their 40 years together, had experienced two world wars. They had talked often about how to prevent another war. These conversations helped to lay the groundwork for the United Nations. In December 1945, President Harry Truman asked Eleanor to be a delegate to the U.N.'s first meeting in London.

Eleanor wrote in her syndicated newspaper column "My Day" on December 21, 1945, "Some things I can take to the first meeting: A sincere desire to understand the problems of the rest of the world and our relationship to them; a real goodwill for people throughout the rest of the world; a hope that I shall be able to build a sense of personal trust and friendship with my co-workers, for without that understanding our work would be doubly difficult."[3]

The next month, she was on her way to England. It was a tremendous responsibility for her. Once, she explained why she studied every paper handed to her regarding the United Nations, saying, "I knew that, if I in any way failed, it would not be just my failure; it would be the failure of all women. There'd never be another woman on the delegation."[4] She was initially assigned to the Social, Humanitarian and Cultural Committee because the men in charge thought she could not do much harm there. As the United Nations became the diplomatic battleground between the Soviet Union and the West, Eleanor's stand on various issues became the talk of the assembly.

"When she got into the brickbats and in-fighting in the U.N. committees and so forth, Eleanor Roosevelt knew how to handle it far better than some of these chaps did," her grandson, Curtis Roosevelt, said.[5] Soon she was elected to chair the committee drafting a Universal Declaration of Human Rights. There was no single concept of what human rights and freedoms meant.

She worked 18 to 20 hours a day on the project, which she was passionately interested in. She hammered away on every item in what was to be a declaration of basic principles

During an informal huddle at the United Nations General Assembly in 1947, Eleanor Roosevelt spoke with Secretary of State George C. Marshall *(right)*. With them was Francis B. Sayre, alternate U.S. delegate to the United Nations. As a U.N. delegate, Eleanor Roosevelt chaired the committee drafting the Universal Declaration of Human Rights.

of human rights, placing special emphasis on discrimination. Originally, the document had started out to say "All men are born free and equal in dignity and rights." Eleanor made sure that the beginning was changed to "All human beings are born free and equal in dignity and rights."[6]

After more than two years of work, the United Nations Universal Declaration of Human Rights was approved on December 10, 1948. Forty-eight nations voted in favor of the declaration; no nations voted against it; and eight nations abstained from voting. Eleanor Roosevelt remained a delegate to the United Nations General Assembly until the end of 1952, when Dwight D. Eisenhower was elected president. Since Eleanor had been appointed by President Truman, she stepped down after Eisenhower's election.

She was 68 years old. She began to travel again, making three trips to Israel over the next 10 years. She also went to Japan, the Soviet Union, and India, and everywhere was greeted as though she were a head of state.

The first volume of her papers, titled *The Human Rights Years, 1945–48*, was published in 2007, and Hillary Rodham Clinton wrote the introduction. *Newsweek* writer Julia Baird, reviewing the book, said she was a "pragmatic, savvy politician," and historian Arthur Schlesinger Jr. good-humoredly labeled her a "tough and salty old lady."[7] Allida Black, the editor of the volume, said that the papers were published because everyone thought of Eleanor as "this great, bleeding liberal conscience who had no experience in crafting hard-nosed realistic policy." Instead, Black said, "She hid behind her traditional image to shape policy."[8]

Throughout these years, many were dependent on Eleanor. She worried about her friend and secretary, Malvina "Tommy" Thompson, who was not well. Her children needed her help, both financially and emotionally, and she continued to be troubled by what she perceived as her failure as a mother. Her sons were in and out of various ventures that did not succeed. Franklin Jr. was like his father in looks and charm. He even sounded like his father. But he was not disciplined. After being elected to Congress in 1949, he spent little time on the job, preferring instead to party in New York. He tried to follow in the footsteps of his father and his Great Uncle Theodore by running for governor of New York, but he lost the nomination. He lost again when he ran for attorney general.

A DEEPER FOCUS ON CIVIL RIGHTS

Eleanor pushed herself, keeping a relentless schedule of meetings and lectures. She grew fiercer as she aged. She openly railed against Senator Joseph McCarthy's anti-Communist crusade. Although the FBI never began a formal investigation against Eleanor Roosevelt, it had compiled a file of more than 3,000 pages on her. FBI director J. Edgar Hoover saw her as a threat to the status quo in the United States because of her association with liberal groups, her outspokenness against segregation and lynching, and her assertions for free speech. Eleanor Roosevelt protested the investigations of her friends and colleagues, but the FBI continued to amass its file until her death.

As great a concern as human rights around the globe was for Eleanor Roosevelt, she placed just as strong an emphasis on the issue of civil rights at home. She joined the NAACP Board of Directors in May 1945 and the Congress on Racial Equality board that same year. She

IN HER OWN WORDS

While some people criticized Eleanor Roosevelt as having Communist sympathies, she fervently believed in our democratic system. In her 1940 book *The Moral Basis of Democracy*, she wrote:

> If we are honest with ourselves today, we will acknowledge that the ideal of democracy has never failed, but that we haven't carried it out, and in our lack of faith we have debased the human being who must have a chance to live if democracy is to be successful.

urged President Truman to address the NAACP's annual convention in 1948 and joined him on the steps of the Lincoln Memorial when he did. Her newspaper column and other writings were tutorials on civil-rights issues. She covered segregated schools, employment discrimination, voting procedures that excluded blacks, and restrictive housing covenants.

She was thrilled when schools had to be integrated after the Supreme Court issued its landmark decision in 1954 in the *Brown v. Board of Education* case. The court's ruling stated that "separate educational facilities are inherently unequal." She worked with Martin Luther King Jr. and Rosa Parks and others to raise money for the Montgomery Bus Boycott, which was a protest against segregation on the public-transit system in Montgomery, Alabama. She supported efforts to desegregate hospitals and protect voting rights. She reminded Americans over and over that it was hypocritical to be critical of Communism but support Jim Crow laws that prevented African Americans from the freedoms that whites took for granted.

In 1958, Roosevelt was to speak at a civil-rights workshop at a school in Tennessee. The day before she was to leave, the FBI contacted her, told her that the Ku Klux Klan had put a bounty on her head, and said the agency could not protect her. Roosevelt went anyway and was met at the Nashville airport by a 71-year-old woman. They got in the car, put a loaded pistol between them, and traveled to the school. There, she conducted a workshop on how to conduct nonviolent civil disobedience.

"She was tough as nails," historian Geoff Ward said. "She had made herself tough. She was just as tough as FDR, just as tough as Theodore Roosevelt."[9]

When the Civil Rights Acts of 1957 and 1960 were being hotly debated, Roosevelt used her column to go after Democrats who tried to evade the issue. She initially

Eleanor Roosevelt joined the board of the NAACP in 1945. Here, she goes over an agenda with NAACP members and executive officers *(from left)* James McClendon, Walter White, Roy Wilkins, and Thurgood Marshall. She remained active in the civil-rights movement during the 1950s.

opposed John F. Kennedy's nomination to be president in 1960 because he was not overtly supporting civil rights.

Her columns grew more pessimistic as she realized the slow progress to a race-blind society. When she learned of the attacks on James Meredith as he became the first African American to enroll at the University of Mississippi in October 1962, she invited Martin Luther King Jr. to appear on her television show, *Prospects of Mankind*, a monthly program she hosted in which leaders and decision makers discussed current issues. Before Dr. King could appear on the show, she had entered the hospital. King wrote later about her, "The impact of her personality and its unwavering devotion to high principle and purpose cannot be contained in a single day or era."[10]

FEMINIST OR NOT

Because she did not overtly support the Equal Rights Amendment, some have refused to call her a feminist. Most, however, feel that her 40-year campaign to advance women politically, economically, and socially is proof enough. Historian Doris Kearns Goodwin ended an article she wrote for *Time* magazine with these words: "The story of her life—her insistence on her right to an identity of her own apart from her husband and her family, her constant struggle against depression and insecurity, her ability to turn her vulnerabilities into strengths—provides an enduring example of a feminist who transcended the dictates of her times to become one of the century's most powerful and effective advocates for social justice."[11]

ACTIVE UNTIL THE END

Roosevelt regularly appeared on television shows during the last 13 years of her life. When she first began to appear on *Meet the Press*, a group of angry women visited the producer and demanded that she be pulled from the show because she was a Communist. The show backed Roosevelt, and she was frequently invited back. During one show in 1956, she questioned whether President Dwight Eisenhower and Vice President Richard Nixon were qualified for a second term in office. On these shows, her good friend Joseph Lash said, "She showed her deadly capacity for setting off dynamite charges while looking and sounding her most grandmotherly."[12]

In 1959, she was appointed a member of the college faculty at Brandeis University, where she taught a course on international organization and law. She was too modest, though, to be called "professor" and told the university

DID YOU KNOW?

Hillary Clinton has said that Eleanor Roosevelt is her personal heroine and role model, and she has admitted having imaginary conversations with Roosevelt, which made Clinton the butt of many jokes.

On October 5, 1996, a statue of Eleanor Roosevelt was unveiled at the southern tip of Riverside Park at 72nd Street in New York City. The statue, by sculptor Penelope Jencks, was the first depiction of an American woman to be specifically commissioned by the city. It shows Roosevelt leaning on a boulder, chin in hand, thinking. She looks strong and intelligent. Thousands were in attendance, including 35 members of the Roosevelt family and Clinton, who was first lady at the time. "When I last spoke to Mrs. Roosevelt, she wanted me to tell all of you how pleased she is by this great, great new statue," Clinton said, her eyes twinkling.*

Clinton and Roosevelt have another unusual connection, too. On May 21, 1945, a month after Franklin D. Roosevelt died, Harold Ickes wrote to Eleanor Roosevelt and asked her to run for the United States Senate from New York. She said no. More than a half-century later, Harold Ickes Jr. urged Clinton to run for the same seat. She accepted the challenge.

---

* "One First Lady Salutes Another at Statue's Unveiling," *The New York Times*, October 6, 1996.

After leaving the White House, Eleanor Roosevelt remained an influential figure in Democratic politics. Here, she addresses the party's 1960 national convention. She was not happy with John F. Kennedy's nomination as the party's presidential candidate until he met with her at Val-Kill Cottage and won her support.

president to list her as a "lecturer." She was a bit daunted by her new position, though she quickly grew popular with the students. "I was a little staggered by this assignment," she said. "I felt sure that many of these young people were better versed in questions of international organization than I was. But at least I could discuss with them the tangled problems of foreign policy."[13] She taught at Brandeis for the rest of her life.

Eleanor Roosevelt continued to be active in Democratic politics. She campaigned rigorously for her friend Adlai Stevenson in the presidential elections of 1952 and 1956. He lost both times, however, to Eisenhower. Initially, she was disappointed that John F. Kennedy had won the Democratic nomination for president in 1960. She thought he was too young and too conservative. Kennedy went to Val-Kill Cottage and spoke with the woman whose support he firmly believed he needed to win the election. At age 76, she agreed to campaign for him. After he became president in 1961, he appointed her to be a delegate to the United Nations again. She also was on the Advisory Council for the Peace Corps and chaired the Presidential Commission on the Status of Women, which Kennedy had created.

ELEANOR'S DEATH

Roosevelt was in constant pain by mid-1962 and discovered after entering the hospital that she had bone marrow tuberculosis, a rare bacterial disease that prevented the bone marrow from making red blood cells. She hated being in the hospital and finally was moved back to her apartment in New York. Friends and family surrounded her. She was ready to die and refused all medication, but the disease dragged on. Finally, on November 7, she died.

After her death, tributes poured in from around the world. Even the Soviet leader, Nikita Khrushchev, sent his condolences. Flags in the United States flew at half-mast, the first time ever to mark the death of a woman. On November 10, 1,000 people went to Hyde Park to bid their farewell.

A Lasting Legacy

How did Eleanor Roosevelt emerge from such a sheltered and sad childhood to become one of the greatest stateswomen of the twentieth century? Archibald MacLeish wrote about that transformation in an article that appeared in *The New York Times* on November 7, 1965, three years after her death. He wrote: "My own notion is that the answer may perhaps be found in the old human wisdom which expresses itself in myths like the myth of the sleeping beauty. People aren't 'made' by themselves or by anyone else. They are released to be what they always were but had never known they were. And what releases them is the touch of life—the 'kiss' of life, the fairy tale would say."[1] He believed that she was first awakened to human suffering when she saw soldiers returning from World War I, and though she seemed to be sleeping for many years, she finally discovered the "freedom and passion of the awakened woman."[2]

Even as a child, Eleanor was introduced to an unusual degree of suffering, from the deaths of family members to the notion that she was always an outsider, and an ugly one at that. After her husband's betrayal, she started to reinvent herself. When polio threatened his life and his career, she became his champion. She slowly developed a philosophy that the best way to alleviate one's own pain is to help others.

Another aspect of her times contributed to Eleanor Roosevelt being a late bloomer—she was born into a society that conditioned women to believe they were second-class citizens. The woman's place was in the home, raising children and keeping house. Even if she had wanted to be a mother and a housekeeper, because of her controlling mother-in-law and the nannies, there was little for her to do.

All the while she fought dark depressions that sometimes incapacitated her. She referred to them as her Griselda moods. "If anyone looks at me, I want to weep," she wrote. "My mind goes round and round like a squirrel in a cage. I want to run and I can't and I despise myself."[3] With therapy and anti-depressants common today, it is difficult to understand the stigma attached to depression back then. Roosevelt would not have considered seeking help for her illness.

For a woman who was intelligent, curious, had tremendous energy, and yet who wanted to conform to keep everyone in the family happy, the frustration must have threatened to overwhelm her. Allida M. Black, who wrote the foreword to a book by one of Eleanor's grandsons titled *Grandmère: A Personal History of Eleanor Roosevelt*, said, "ER led a full but difficult life defined by conflict and disappointment while empowered by duty and vision."[4] Once she entered politics, she was constantly balancing her multiple roles against the expectations of family and friends. This is the norm for women today, but Eleanor Roosevelt was a pioneer in becoming an independent woman.

Her transformation from shy and unhappy wife and hostess to writer and diplomat has fascinated more than one writer. James MacGregor Burns and Janet Thompson Burns wrote about the changes they had observed in a *New York Times* article that appeared on Roosevelt's seventy-fifth birthday: "One senses that time has both strengthened and hardened her. Certainly this outwardly poised, dominating woman is almost a totally different person today from the timid fiancée of 1903."[5] She was also not the person she was when she was first lady, the woman who was a combination of wife, critic, and confidante. She had become a force in her own right. The Burnses wrote, "The balance between pragmatism and idealism that once existed between her and her husband now operates within Eleanor Roosevelt herself."[6]

At the time of her death, Roosevelt was the most recognized woman in the world. The face that made her wince in her youth made her a perfect target for caricaturists, but in her later years it was that same face that exuded attentiveness, curiosity, and compassion. People were drawn to her, and trusted her. She was ranked the "World's Most Popular Woman" for 15 consecutive years in a Gallup poll, and is today Gallup's ninth most admired person in the twentieth century.

She singlehandedly created a new role for the first lady and went on to a distinguished career after FDR's death. She withstood extreme criticism and even had threats made on her life, but she chose to ignore them. It was as a United Nations delegate that she made her mark, drawing up the Universal Declaration of Human Rights. Her work to pass civil-rights legislation was equally important, but it took longer to achieve results.

Eleanor Roosevelt talked with guests during a get-together at her home at Val-Kill in 1957. Her transformation from a mousy, dependent wife into a vibrant public figure and activist continues to captivate people.

She acquired a political wisdom that could be put to good use today. A collection of her monthly magazine question-and-answer pieces titled "If You Ask Me" was published. Asked which she thought was more important, that a president be a master of politics or a master of administration, she answered, "I think the percentage should probably be fifty-fifty. One test is left out, however, which I think is perhaps one of the most important. A man may be a good administrator and a good politician and still not have the understanding heart which is essential, I think, to be a good servant of the people."[7]

She was emphatic that Americans must stop thinking of the struggle between Communism and democracy as purely military, a reasoning that could be applied to the Middle East today. She felt that the United States was overemphasizing the military even then. She stressed the importance of electing responsible people who would answer to their constituents as a whole and not to the leader of a political party alone.

Were she alive today, she would not be silent. She would be speaking about the war in Iraq and the politics of fear. In a 2007 *Newsweek* article titled "The Savvy, Salty Political Saint," Julia Baird wrote, "We are living in a world indelibly shaped by her. If we fail to recognize how much more than a 'well-protected flower' she was, then she is simply continuing to outfox us all."[8]

In an earlier article for *The New York Times*, MacLeish wrote, "Only rarely does a great name grow greater when its owner leaves it, as Eleanor Roosevelt's unquestionably does. The center of her concern was the struggle for human dignity."[9] She played an active role in many causes during her lifetime, but, MacLeish wrote, "It was the long fight for a meaningful and common freedom that had her first and last commitment, and it is there that her voice and her presence are still most powerfully felt."[10]

CHRONOLOGY

1884   Born on October 11 in New York City.

1892   Her mother, Anna Hall Roosevelt, dies, and her maternal grandmother, Mary Hall, assumes responsibility for her care.

1894   Her father, Elliott, dies from alcoholism.

1899   Enrolls at Allenswood School in England.

1902   Leaves Allenswood and makes her debut in New York City.

1903   Becomes engaged to Franklin Delano Roosevelt; joins the Junior League and volunteers at Rivington Street College Settlement.

1905   Marries Franklin D. Roosevelt on March 17 in New York.

1906   Gives birth to Anna.

1907   Gives birth to James.

1909   Gives birth to Franklin D. Roosevelt Jr., who dies of influenza when seven months old.

1910   Gives birth to Elliott; Franklin Roosevelt is elected to the New York State Senate, and the family moves to Albany, New York.

1913   Franklin Roosevelt is appointed assistant secretary of the Navy, and the family moves to Washington, D.C.

1914   Gives birth to a son, also named Franklin D. Roosevelt Jr.

1916   Gives birth to John.

1918   Eleanor Roosevelt learns of the affair between Franklin Roosevelt and Lucy Mercer; she decides not to divorce her husband after he agrees never to see Mercer again.

1920   Travels with her husband after he wins the Democratic nomination for vice president of the United States.

1921   Franklin Roosevelt is stricken with polio.

1922   Meets Nancy Cook and Marion Dickerman.

1924   Wins fight to allow women to name the female delegates to the New York State Democratic Convention.

1925   Builds Val-Kill Cottage with her husband and Cook and Dickerman.

1928   Franklin Roosevelt is elected governor of New York.

1929   Earl Miller becomes her bodyguard; Eleanor hires Malvina "Tommy" Thompson to be her secretary, a position Thompson held until her death in 1953.

1932   Franklin Roosevelt is elected president of the United States.

1933   Begins to hold press conferences—a first for a first lady; New Deal programs start to be implemented.

1936   Franklin Roosevelt is reelected president.

1939   Arranges for African-American singer Marian Anderson to sing at the Lincoln Memorial after the Daughters of the American Revolution banned her from performing at Constitution Hall.

1940   Addresses the Democratic National Convention on behalf of FDR's choice of vice president; FDR is reelected to an unprecedented third term as president.

1941   Eleanor Roosevelt begins to serve as assistant director of the Office of Civilian Defense.

1942   Resigns from her position with OCD.

1943   Tours South Pacific to encourage troops and visit with wounded soldiers.

1944   Franklin Roosevelt is elected to a fourth term as president.

1945 Franklin Roosevelt dies on April 12 in Warm Springs, Georgia; Eleanor Roosevelt joins the board of directors of the NAACP; she is appointed as a delegate to the United Nations by President Harry Truman.

1946 Chairs the United Nations Human Rights Commission, which creates the Universal Declaration of Human Rights.

1948 The U.N. General Assembly adopts the Universal Declaration of Human Rights.

1952 Resigns as a delegate to the United Nations.

1955 Supports the Montgomery Bus Boycott.

1959 Begins TV interview show, *Prospects of Mankind*; becomes a lecturer at Brandeis University.

1961 Reappointed as a delegate to the United Nations by President John Kennedy; chairs the Presidential Commission on the Status of Women.

1962 Dies on November 7 in New York at the age of 78.

NOTES

CHAPTER 1: FINDING HER VOICE AT 60

1. Eleanor Roosevelt, *The Autobiography of Eleanor Roosevelt*, New York: De Capo Press, 1961, p. 276.
2. Joseph P. Lash, *Eleanor and Franklin*, New York: W.W. Norton & Company Inc., 1971, p. 237.
3. Doris Kearns Goodwin, "Eleanor Roosevelt," *Time*, April 13, 1998. Available online at http://www.time.com/time/time100/leaders/profile/eleanor.html.
4. Blanche Wiesen Cook, *Eleanor Roosevelt, Vol. 2: 1933–1938*, New York: Penguin Books, 1999, p. 30.
5. Ibid., p. 552.
6. Joseph P. Lash, *Eleanor: The Years Alone*, New York: W.W. Norton, 1972, p. 26.
7. Roosevelt, *The Autobiography of Eleanor Roosevelt*, p. 280.

CHAPTER 2: A STORM-TOSSED CHILDHOOD

1. Blanche Wiesen Cook, *Eleanor Roosevelt, Vol. 1: 1884–1933*, New York: Penguin Books, 1992, p. 62.
2. Ibid., p. 71.
3. Ibid., p. 78.
4. Ibid., p. 92.
5. Roosevelt, *The Autobiography of Eleanor Roosevelt*, p. 13.
6. Candace Fleming, *Our Eleanor: A Scrapbook Look at Eleanor Roosevelt's Remarkable Life*, New York: Atheneum Books for Young Readers, 2005, p. 12.

CHAPTER 3: THE TEEN YEARS

1. Roosevelt, *The Autobiography of Eleanor Roosevelt*, p. 412.
2. Lash, *Eleanor and Franklin*, p. 75.
3. Cook, *Eleanor Roosevelt, Vol. 1*, pp. 120–121.
4. Ibid., p. 126.
5. Ibid., p. 129.
6. Ibid., p. 130
7. Ibid., p. 132.
8. Ibid., p. 139.
9. Ibid., p. 147.
10. Ibid., p. 148.

11. Ibid., p. 153.
12. Ibid., p. 154.

CHAPTER 4: MARRIAGE TO FRANKLIN ROOSEVELT

1. Ibid., p. 167.
2. Ibid., p. 187.
3. Ibid., p. 200.

CHAPTER 5: LIFE-CHANGING EVENTS

1. Ibid., p. 203.
2. Ibid., p. 214.
3. Joseph Alsop, *FDR: A Centenary Remembrance*, New York: The Viking Press, 1982.
4. Cook, *Eleanor Roosevelt, Vol. 1*, p. 224.
5. Ibid., p. 234.
6. Ibid., p. 237.
7. Ibid., p. 250.
8. *American Experience: Eleanor Roosevelt*. Ambrica Productions Inc. and WGBH Educational Foundation, 2000. Transcript available at http://www.pbs.org/wgbh/amex/eleanor/filmmore/transcript/transcript1.htm.

CHAPTER 6: REINVENTING ELEANOR

1. *American Experience: The Presidents—FDR*. WGBH Educational Foundation and David Grubin Productions Inc., 1994. Transcript available at http://www.pbs.org/wgbh/amex/presidents/32_f_roosevelt/filmmore/filmscript.html.
2. Ibid.
3. Cook. *Eleanor Roosevelt, Vol. 1*, p. 313.
4. *American Experience: Eleanor Roosevelt*.
5. Cook, *Eleanor Roosevelt, Vol. 1*, p. 348.
6. Fleming, *Our Eleanor*, p. 62.
7. *American Experience: The Presidents—FDR*.

CHAPTER 7: REVOLUTIONIZING THE ROLE OF THE FIRST LADY

1. *American Experience: Eleanor Roosevelt.*
2. Ibid.
3. *American Experience: The Presidents—FDR.*
4. Ibid.
5. Fleming, *Our Eleanor*, p. 90.
6. Ibid., p. 90.
7. Ibid., p. 12.
8. Ibid., p. 112.
9. *American Experience: Eleanor Roosevelt.*

CHAPTER 8: THE WAR YEARS

1. Fleming, *Our Eleanor*, p. 104.
2. Ibid., p. 115.
3. Goodwin, "Eleanor Roosevelt," *Time.*
4. Susan M. Hartmann, *The Home Front and Beyond: American Women in the 1940s*, New York: Macmillan, 1984.
5. *American Experience: Eleanor Roosevelt.*
6. Fleming, *Our Eleanor*, p. 124.
7. Ibid., p. 124.
8. Ibid., p. 126
9. Ibid., p. 128.
10. David M. Kennedy, "Affairs Both Foreign and Domestic," *New York Times*, September 11, 1994.
11. Fleming, *Our Eleanor*, p. 127.
12. Kennedy, "Affairs Both Foreign and Domestic."
13. Fleming, *Our Eleanor*, p. 129.

CHAPTER 9: FIRST LADY OF THE WORLD

1. Goodwin, "Eleanor Roosevelt," *Time.*
2. Fleming, *Our Eleanor*, p. 130.
3. Ibid., p. 135.
4. Ibid., p. 135.
5. *American Experience: Eleanor Roosevelt.*

6. Ibid.
7. Julia Baird, "The Savvy, Salty Political Saint," *Newsweek*, December 15, 2007. Available online at http://www.newsweek.com/id/78177.
8. Ibid.
9. *American Experience: Eleanor Roosevelt.*
10. "Eleanor Roosevelt and Civil Rights," Eleanor Roosevelt National Historical Site Web site. Available online at http://www.nps.gov/archive/elro/teach-er-vk/lesson-plans/notes-er-and-civil-rights.htm.
11. Goodwin, "Eleanor Roosevelt," *Time.*
12. Fleming, *Our Eleanor*, p. 148.
13. Roosevelt, *The Autobiography of Eleanor Roosevelt*, p. 405.

CHAPTER 10: A LASTING LEGACY
1. Archibald MacLeish, "Eleanor Roosevelt: The Awakening," *New York Times*, November 7, 1965.
2. Ibid.
3. Fleming, *Our Eleanor*, p. 25.
4. Allida M. Black, foreword, *Grandmère: A Personal History of Eleanor Roosevelt*, by David B. Roosevelt, New York: Warner Books, 2002, p. vi.
5. James MacGregor Burns and Janet Thompson Burns, "Mrs. Roosevelt at a Remarkable 75," *New York Times*, October 4, 1959.
6. Ibid.
7. Lucy Greenbaum, "The Opinions of Eleanor Roosevelt," *New York Times*, April 28, 1946.
8. Baird, "The Savvy, Salty Political Saint."
9. Archibald MacLeish, "Tribute to a 'Great American Lady,'" *New York Times*, November 3, 1962.
10. Ibid.

BIBLIOGRAPHY

Alsop, Joseph. *FDR: A Centenary Remembrance*. New York: The Viking Press, 1982.

American Experience: Eleanor Roosevelt. Ambrica Productions Inc. and WGBH Educational Foundation, 2000. Transcript available at http://www.pbs.org/wgbh/amex/eleanor/filmmore/transcript/transcript1.htm.

American Experience: The Presidents—FDR. WGBH Educational Foundation and David Grubin Productions Inc., 1994. Transcript available at http://www.pbs.org/wgbh/amex/presidents/32_f_roosevelt/filmmore/filmscript.html.

Baird, Julia. "The Savvy, Salty Political Saint," *Newsweek*, December 15, 2007. Available online at http://www.newsweek.com/id/78177.

Burns, James MacGregor, and Janet Thompson Burns. "Mrs. Roosevelt at a Remarkable 75," *New York Times*, October 4, 1959.

Cook, Blanche Wiesen. *Eleanor Roosevelt, Vol. 1: 1884–1933*. New York: Penguin Books, 1992.

———. *Eleanor Roosevelt, Vol. 2: 1933–1938*. New York: Penguin Books, 1999.

"Eleanor Roosevelt and Civil Rights," Eleanor Roosevelt National Historical Site Web site. Available online at http://www.nps.gov/archive/elro/teach-er-vk/lesson-plans/notes-er-and-civil-rights.htm.

Fleming, Candace. *Our Eleanor: A Scrapbook Look at Eleanor Roosevelt's Remarkable Life*. New York: Atheneum Books for Young Readers, 2005.

Goodwin, Doris Kearns. "Eleanor Roosevelt." *Time*, April 13, 1998. Available online at http://www.time.com/time/time100/leaders/profile/eleanor.html.

Greenbaum, Lucy. "The Opinions of Eleanor Roosevelt." *New York Times*, April 28, 1946.

Kennedy, David M. "Affairs Both Foreign and Domestic," *New York Times*, September 11, 1994.

Lash, Joseph P. *Eleanor and Franklin*. New York: W.W. Norton & Company, Inc., 1971.

———. *Eleanor: The Years Alone*. New York: W.W. Norton, 1972.

MacLeish, Archibald. "Eleanor Roosevelt: The Awakening," *New York Times*, November 7, 1965.

———. "Tribute to a 'Great American Lady.'" *New York Times*, November 3, 1962.

Roosevelt, David B. *Grandmère: A Personal History of Eleanor Roosevelt*. New York: Warner Books, 2002.

Roosevelt, Eleanor. *The Autobiography of Eleanor Roosevelt*. New York: De Capo Press, 1961.

FURTHER RESOURCES

BOOKS

Emblidge, David, ed. *My Day: The Best of Eleanor Roosevelt's Acclaimed Newspaper Columns, 1936–1962.* New York: DeCapo Press, 2001.

Glendon, Mary Ann. *A World Made New: Eleanor Roosevelt and the Universal Declaration of Human Rights.* New York: Random House, 2002.

Gurewitsch, Edna P. *Kindred Souls: The Friendship of Eleanor Roosevelt and David Gurewitsch.* New York: St. Martin's Press, 2002.

Roosevelt, Eleanor. *You Learn by Living: Eleven Keys for a More Fulfilling Life.* Louisville, Kentucky: Westminster John Knox Press, 1960.

WEB SITES

American Experience: Eleanor Roosevelt
http://www.pbs.org/wgbh/amex/eleanor

Eleanor Roosevelt
http://www.udhr.org/history/Biographies/bioer.htm

The Eleanor Roosevelt Papers Project
http://www.gwu.edu/~erpapers/

Franklin D. Roosevelt Presidential Library and Museum
http://www.fdrlibrary.marist.edu

New Deal Network
http://newdeal.feri.org

INDEX

ABOUT THE AUTHOR

JANET HUBBARD-BROWN has written extensively for Chelsea House Publishers, including biographies on Shirin Ebadi, who won the Nobel Peace Prize in 2003, and Condoleezza Rice. A resident of Vermont, Hubbard-Brown writes for various magazines there and teaches writing in Fayston, Vermont.

PICTURE CREDITS

Page